WITH BEST WISHES,

Bill

DOIN' DRUGS

DOIN' DRUGS

Patterns of African American Addiction

William H. James and
Stephen L. Johnson

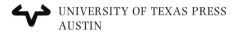
UNIVERSITY OF TEXAS PRESS
AUSTIN

Requests for permission to reproduce material from this work
should be sent to Permissions, University of Texas Press,
Box 7819, Austin, TX 78713-7819.

⊗ The paper used in this publication meets the minimum
requirements of American National Standard for Information
Sciences—Permanence of Paper for Printed Library Materials,
ANSI Z39.48-1984.

Library of Congress Cataloging-in-Publication Data

James, William H. (William Henry), 1940–
    Doin' Drugs : patterns of African American addiction / by
William H. James and Stephen L. Johnson.
        p.   cm.
    Includes bibliographical references and index.
    ISBN 0-292-74040-9 (cloth : alk. paper). — ISBN 0-292-74041-7
(pbk. : alk. paper)
    1. Afro-Americans—Drug use.   2. Afro-Americans—Alcohol
use.   3. Afro-Americans—Social conditions.   4. Narcotic
addicts—Rehabilitation—United States.   5. Alcoholics—
Rehabilitation—United States.   6. Drug abuse—Treatment—
United States.   7. Alcoholism—Treatment—United States.
I. Johnson, Stephen L. (Stephen Lloyd)   II. Title.
HV5824.E85J36   1996
362.29'12'08996073—dc20   96-16400

This book is dedicated with love to
African Americans in recovery who have told their
stories so that others may begin the process of
hope, healing, and recovery.

CONTENTS

Illustrations follow page xi.

PREFACE

During the 1980s crack cocaine use by African Americans grew so dramatically that most African American communities were in their second decade of a crack cocaine epidemic in the 1990s. The marketing of highly addictive, low-cost "crack" has changed the very fabric of urban African American life. Increased crime, prostitution, and gang violence has resulted in a "War on Drugs," which has more often appeared to be a war on addicts. Thousands of African American men remain in prison for drug charges that in the white community may have resulted in no more than a fine, probation, or community service.

The ability of African American communities to confront this crack cocaine epidemic will determine the character of African American urban life well into the next century. Traditional alcohol and other drug treatment programs have been unable to stop the wave of addiction that has engulfed the African American community. A coalition of the strongest resources in these communities, including families, churches, schools, and community agencies, is urgently needed to address such widespread drug use.

In the United States drug addiction has been portrayed as a Chinese menace, or an African American problem, or a Latin American problem. Periodically different racial and ethnic groups have been stigmatized and held responsible for the ongoing drug crisis American society has experienced. This book has not been written to scapegoat the African American community with responsibility for drug use in America. It has been written in the belief that an accurate portrayal of the present and historic realities of African American addiction will help African American leaders, communities, churches, and colleges and universities meet the challenges of urban addiction.

Doin' Drugs: Patterns of African American Addiction attempts to capture the historic and modern patterns of African American addiction and alcoholism so that the interplay of addiction and race might be better understood. It is our hope that, in doing this, the book will be used to better prepare a new generation of counselors, ministers, social workers, nurses, and physicians to face the epidemic of drug addiction in African American communities.

Most drug treatment programs are designed by individuals in recovery who replicate the approach that worked for them. Some programs take a shotgun approach and say that "a drug is a drug is a drug." Other programs focus on treating individuals at different stages in the progression of their addictive diseases. Few programs ask the deeper questions: What is a good recovery program for this particular racial, age, or gender group? What are the best learning styles for African Americans in recovery? What strengths do African Americans bring to a recovery program that will help us understand how to design a program for them?

We started the Cocaine Outreach and Recovery Program (CORP) of Seattle in 1989 specifically to treat crack cocaine addiction in cocaine-dependent African Americans. In developing the agency we asked ourselves: How can we develop a program for cocaine-using African American males and females, their families, and their communities? What values, beliefs, norms of behaviors, mores, experiences, interests, and abilities do they have that will inform our program development? What treatment philosophy will assist these men and women in gaining long-term recovery?

At the heart of our treatment philosophy is the belief that a drug treatment program based on compliance is counterproductive for African Americans. African Americans were brought to this country as slaves and were kept in this compliant situation as an unpaid labor force for three centuries. Currently, approximately 33 percent of young African Americans are in jail, on parole, or supervised in some way by the corrections system. We believe that the heart of an effective treatment philosophy for cocaine addiction in African Americans is the encouragement of voluntary involvement. When creating the program, we recognized the importance of autonomy, dignity, and pride in the African American culture, and we work hard to not do the planning, thinking, and decision making that African Americans in recovery can do for themselves. Authoritarian and rigid decision making by staff will elicit rebellious behavior and needlessly result in failure to complete the program. We do not believe in discharging clients after one relapse, for they are struggling with a powerful addiction that is very complex and difficult to deal with. The practice of discharging after a single relapse, which many programs follow, seems only to enlarge the pool of African Americans who feel like failures. We believe in empowerment and mutual decision making; we seek to help light the fires of self-concern, pride, and development.

Our underlying philosophy utilizes the bonding needs that have been at the root of male-dominated societies in Africa as well as gangs in this country. Too often treatment programs focus on individual effort and ignore treatment group relationships. Most crack-addicted males at CORP come into recovery having had little experience with friendship and mutual support. Most crack-addicted females come in as victims of sexual exploitation and other forms of victimization. African American heritage encourages traits like loyalty, honesty, and trust, but we find that our men have not known much real caring and support from other men, nor do women experience such caring and support from other women. At CORP we help men and women move into a belonging relationship with other members and with the program. CORP participants are called "members" rather than "clients" in order to promote the group connection. Individuals need to move into recovery together. As one man in our program recently observed, "It's an *us* thing, not a *me* thing."

Top, Leonard Irvin, CORP board member, at the 1994 Solutions to Neighbor-hood Violence conference, Mt. Zion Baptist Church, Seattle. (Photo by Kameron Durham.) *Middle left*, Rev. Michael Booker and Rev. Toni Booker at the 1991 PNW conference on crack cocaine. (Photo by Kameron Durham.) *Middle right*, Rev. Stephen L. Johnson at the Solutions to Neighborhood Violence conference. (Photo by Kameron Durham.) *Bottom*, William H. James with members of CORP's Women's Program. (Photo courtesy of Rev. Stephen L. Johnson.)

ACKNOWLEDGMENTS

For nearly two years this book has been our focus of research, travel, analysis, and writing. Our research effort has required continual intellectual and moral support, and we have been blessed to have so many willing to assist us with this project.

No one contributed more to the development of this book than the members of the Cocaine Outreach and Recovery Program. The research involved in writing this book is connected to African American people who are struggling to find hope, healing, and recovery from the disease of chemical dependency. At the Program we were assisted by members whose honesty and openness about their addiction added invaluable insights to this manuscript. They also contributed to numerous interviews, while offering thoughts and experiences critical to the construction of the book. We appreciate the willingness of the young African Americans confined to juvenile detention who consented to talk with us about their drug use and gang involvement. We also wish to recognize those individuals in recovery from drug use that we interviewed in programs in Seattle, San Francisco, Atlanta, Philadelphia, and New York City.

As we put this research into book form we were fortunate to have the assistance of two excellent editors. Beginning with the early drafts, Theresa May at the University of Texas Press provided the initial editing and intellectual support that facilitated the literary quality of the book. At the same time we received constant encouragement and direction from Lois Rankin at the Press, who provided the detailed reading, analysis, and editing needed for the manuscript.

For their steady assistance and support throughout the research and writing of this book, we also thank the staff of the Alcohol and Drug Abuse Institute, a research center at the University of Washington, and the College of Education. We are particularly grateful to Dr. Barbara Wallace at Columbia University, Dr. David Moore at Olympic Counseling Services, and Dr. John Wallace for their constant intellectual contributions and moral support, as well as that offered by our friends and families.

We received much-needed spiritual support and blessings from the Reverend Samuel Berry McKinney at Mt. Zion Baptist Church in Seattle and from the Reverend Cecil Williams at Glide Memorial Methodist Church in San Francisco. In Philadelphia the Reverend Arlene Churn provided guidance, insight, and warm support.

Given the nature of this book, it was critical to gain the insights of those with particular knowledge of each drug and its impact on African Americans. For the chapter on alcohol use, we are especially grateful to several war veterans and members of Alcoholics Anonymous for sharing their experiences from the 1950s onward. The chapter on cigarettes and marijuana and that on gangs were greatly enhanced by the help given to us by young people in public school or juvenile detention and by members of Marijuana Anonymous. For the chapters on opium and cocaine, we owe a debt of gratitude to members of Cocaine Anonymous and Narcotics Anonymous groups and those African Americans who consented to interviews for our research.

These acknowledgments barely reach the many African American individuals and families who helped with this project. But at the end of the process, we feel the most gratitude for our families, who stood by us throughout the length of the project. In this regard, we would like to thank especially Phyllis Johnson-Schmidt, mother of Stephen Lloyd Johnson, and Cleo Molina, wife of William Henry James, for putting up with us through this both arduous and exciting project. Without our family support, we probably would have abandoned this project at one of the numerous turns in the road on the way to completion.

DOIN' DRUGS

1 HISTORICAL PATTERNS OF ALCOHOL AND DRUG USE

They that sow in tears shall reap in joy.

—Psalm 126:5

African American addiction is often evaluated without a close examination of the traditional uses of alcohol and drugs in Africa and without an understanding of the trauma African people suffered when separated from their ancestors, religion, and homeland. Certainly, it is important to keep in mind that slaves did not come to the Americas from a social or religious void, and thus they brought with them highly evolved patterns of drug and alcohol use for religious, social, and medical purposes.

ALCOHOL AND DRUG USE IN AFRICA

The first European traffic in African slaves began in Seville, Spain, between 1399 and 1442 (Cobb 1858), well before Columbus's discovery of the New World. As early as 1501 slaves captured by the Portuguese in the Lagos, Nigeria, region were sent to the West Indies, and in 1562 to England. Slaves continued to be shipped primarily from West Africa—from Senegal in the North to Angola in the South. Many of the tribal groups severely affected by slavery were recovering from devastating internal conflicts and war with neighboring nations (Davidson 1966).

Some captives, despairing of ever returning to their homeland, chose death rather than give in to their captivity.

The slaves arriving in America came from such tribes as the Mandingos, Koromantyns, Whidahs, Fidahs, Eboes, and Congoes, tribes familiar with fermented maize or millet as a foodstuff, a trade product, an important part of social interaction, and a sacred drink. Wine made from locally tapped palm trees was used by many tribes for social and religious ceremonies, and numerous African cultures brewed beer, the drinking of which was "an integral part of virtually any social interchange among men in most African tribal societies" (Heath 1975: 15). Beer was and continues to be used "[as an offering] to gods and spirits, as a pledge of agreement between parties following adjudication, [and] as a token of appreciation to those who have taken turns working one's land" (ibid.).

Studies have focused on the presence of alcohol and other drugs in specific areas of Africa and on the role of these drugs in the long history of trading relations between the West African coast and Europe—for example, the trade between Europeans (who first wanted slaves, and then palm oil) and the Ijaw-Nembe, Kalabari, Bonny, and Opobo, a trade relationship begun by the Portuguese in the fifteenth century and continued by the British. European contact with the Kofyar, farmers occupying an area in northern Nigeria, began in 1909, when the British established control of the land. However, they did not introduce the use of alcohol, for there are indications that the Kofyar brewed beer as a part of their culture and trade before European contact with them (Netting 1964). The Kaguru, a tribe in east-central Tanganyika [now called Tanzania], still brew beer from maize, sugar, or millet throughout the year, and there, too, the practice has historical roots that predate European contact (Beidelman 1961).

Robert McC. Netting, in his anthropological review of the Kofyar, suggests that societies that have well-established drinking patterns in which alcohol has become a focus of group interest also have a minimal amount of disruptive behavior related to alcohol use. The Kofyarian society is well organized around beer drinking:

> The Kofyar make, drink, talk, and think about beer. It is a focus of
> cultural concern and activity in much the same ways as cows . . .
> Among equals, the presenting of beer is a mark of esteem and
> affection. A jar will be saved for a close friend, and institutionalized

friendship among male contemporaries is by means of a named drinking society. Beer is given during courtship by a man to a woman, and the public exchange of beer is typical of lovers in the licit extra-marital relationship. . . . To celebrate the harvest, beer is made by individuals or by popular subscription and distributed freely . . . Major entertainment dances such as the great flute chorus (*koem*) require a large supply of beer . . . A man who exemplifies warrior virtues by killing an enemy or bringing down dangerous game on the hunt is honored by a beer feast and the coveted right to drink from a special reserved fermenting jar at funerals for the rest of his life. (1964: 376)

Netting also suggests that beer in Kofyarian society is used as a social lubricant. Because Kofyarian drinking is a group activity that is defined by distinctive social situations—such as harvest time, parties, and musical events—it is an inclusive rather than exclusive community activity. Individuals do not drink alone, and the possibilities for using beer for private psychological purposes are minimal. The particular Nigerian community Netting describes produced over 83.5 pounds of millet for each household member. This amount of millet provides the equivalent of 40 gallons of beer a year per person. The alcohol content of the beer ranges between 3 and 5 percent, and the average adult drinks between one and two quarts at each drinking party and special event, which occur about twice each week.

The activities of European merchants among the Ijaw of the Delta area of southern Nigeria illustrate the negative impact of the colonial presence on traditional patterns of alcohol use. There the Portuguese originally paid for slaves with cases of gin (which remained a medium of exchange along with other trade goods until British rule in the 1930s). Eventually gin, an alcohol product not even known in traditional village life, replaced palm oil as the main source of village income. By 1958, half the men in the area were involved in the distilling and exporting of gin made from palm wine. The negative effects on the moral life of the community were many, among them engaging in illegal activities such as smuggling gin to get the best price (Leis 1964: 832).

In the same way, the liquor traffic carried on by the United States and Great Britain in Africa as part of slave trading was the "curse of millions" (Kletzing and Crogman 1903). The very vessels that transported missionaries to the shores of Africa also carried thousands of gallons of rum to African ports. The strength of distilled rum was many times that of the beers and wines traditionally consumed in African societies. Accustomed to the use of alcohol in moderation, Africans were severely affected by the introduction of European rum and whiskey, as well as the brewing techniques that produced them.

The use of nonalcoholic drugs in Africa also has a long history. Brian du Toit (1991) in his review of drug use in Africa suggests that most tribal groups south of the Sahara became familiar with marijuana and hashish hundreds of years ago when Arab traders and neighboring tribes introduced *ganja* products and practices as they moved south through the African continent. Early European observers misidentified many African herbs, among them cannabis (marijuana): Western explorers often believed they had found a new drug when in reality they had simply encountered the same cannabis prepared in a different manner or called by a different name. This is not to say that tribal groups in sub-Saharan Africa used cannabis exclusively, for they were familiar with a wide variety of mind-altering herbs, some of which are still in use today.

The famous explorer Dr. David Livingstone, in his 1865 account of his African travels, observed the smoking of cannabis among the Sotho people. Members of this tribe were provided with

> . . . a calabash of pure water, a split bamboo, five feet long, and the great pipe, which has a large calabash or kudu's horn chamber to contain the water, through which the smoke is drawn Narghille fashion, on its way to the mouth. Each smoker takes a few whiffs, the last being an extra long one, and hands the pipe to his neighbor. He seems to swallow the fumes; for, striving against the convulsive action of the muscles of chest and throat, he takes a mouthful of water from the calabash, waits a few seconds, and then pours water and smoke from his mouth down the groove of the bamboo. The smoke causes violent coughing in all, and in some a species of frenzy which passes away in a rapid stream of unmeaning words, or short sentences, as "the green grass grows," "the fat cattle thrive," "the fish swim." (286–287)

Livingstone, who also observed Zulu warriors smoking cannabis before battle, said that they "sat down and smoked it, in order that they might make an effective onslaught" (540).

In 1652, when Europeans arrived at the Cape, they reported wide use of cannabis, as du Toit relates: "When Europeans under the Dutch East Indies Company settled at the Cape in 1652, cannabis already was smoked by indigenous groups, including the Khoikhoi, San, and Bantu speakers" (1991: 17). The first Portuguese observers were confused by various preparations that were eaten or drunk (and did not contain cannabis), preparations that were smoked in various mixtures (which included cannabis), and products that were smelled and inhaled (that might have included cannabis but were usually restricted to roots such as the *gannabossie*, the Ganna shrub). Jan van Riebeeck, the first Dutch commander of the Cape, noted substances that were inhaled, smoked, and drunk. These included the Ganna shrub, as well as cannabis (du Toit 1991).

As scholars address the non-Western interactions that have played a role in forming African culture, the importance of Muslim and Arabic influence in social and religious practices is being better understood. Both Arabian culture and the cultures of northeast and East Africa have had a significant impact on patterns of drug use in Africa. The cultivation and export of *qat*, a leaf that acts as a stimulant, was well established by the middle of the fourteenth century in Yemen (southwestern Arabia) and Ethiopia (northeastern Africa). Shelagh Weir (1985) traces the historic use of this drug in these areas, as well as its widespread use in areas of Somalia and Kenya prior to European rule.

Qat is chewed in North Africa and East Africa and brewed in the form of a tea in the country of South Africa. An evergreen shrub of the plant family Celastraceae, qat is found in Kenya, South Africa, Zaire, Burundi, Rwanda, Uganda, Turkestan, Afghanistan, Tanzania, Zambia, and Mozambique. Fourteenth- and fifteenth-century texts by Muslim scholars have led to a belief that use of this drug was widespread at that time, at least in the Red Sea area. Its present epidemic use in Kenya, Somalia, Ethiopia, and the two Yemens indicates a steady growth in its cultivation and exportation, as well as growing social acceptance of its use.

Accounts from the sixteenth century to eighteenth century, then, clearly indicate that West Africans and East Central Africans had extensive experience with the brewing of beer and wine from grains and fruits, and that southern Africans had some experience with cannabis (marijuana). In African tribal society, the drinking of alcohol was more of a group activity than an individual practice. African religious and sacred events always involved alcohol, except when the tribal member had converted to the Muslim faith. The use of alcohol products had become an integral part of tribal culture, with established norms regarding the use or abuse of these products. Traditional medical practices included the use of palm wine, millet beer, cannabis, as well as more esoteric herbal hallucinatory and nonhallucinatory medications.

ALCOHOL USE DURING THE SLAVERY PERIOD

Many slaves newly arrived in the Americas were proficient at the brewing of maize- and millet-based beers, and they adapted these skills to a variety of agricultural products and social situations they encountered in their new surroundings. Persimmon beer and beer brewed from corn were just two of the products developed by slaves that became popular in the developing colonies. The slaves also drew on the medical and religious uses of alcohol that were a part of their African heritage. Receiving little formal medical care, they turned to the herbal religious healing traditions with which their tribes were familiar in order to survive in their new world.

The first slaves were brought to Jamestown, Virginia, by a Dutch trading vessel in 1619, when twenty slaves were traded for food and supplies. By 1661 the shortage of labor experienced by the early European settlers and explorers led to the passage of laws that legalized slavery. Slaves had no personal rights and by law were doomed to servitude and ignorance (Kletzing and Crogman 1903: 39). Indentured servants were placed in a modified form of slavery which offered the possibility of freedom after a period of service.

By the 1700s, New England, Africa, and the West Indies had entered into a trade triangle. Sugar and molasses from the British and Spanish West Indies were shipped to New England, where it was distilled into rum. The rum was transported to Africa and exchanged for slaves (20 gallons of rum could purchase a muscular young male, and females could be bought for less [Larkins 1965]). These slaves were shipped by merchants to the West Indies to work the fields, completing the economic triangle (Asbury 1950).

Population figures are not available for the early years of slavery but by the first census of the United States (1791), the number of slaves was 587,236, nearly 92 percent of them in the border and southern states and about 8 percent in the Western Territory. The growth of slavery had always been limited in the North—Vermont, New Hampshire,

Maine, Massachusetts, Rhode Island, Connecticut, New York, New Jersey, Pennsylvania, and Delaware—because of climate and soil conditions unfavorable to large-scale agricultural production, the industrial development of the area, and the view held by some that slavery was a wicked and hateful institution. The use of large numbers of slaves for the production of such crops as apples, potatoes, or corn simply was not practical or economically profitable. However, the slave trade in the southern states of Kentucky, North Carolina, South Carolina, and Georgia—and the border states of Maryland and Virginia—flourished because the economy was based on cotton and tobacco, which required intensive labor in order to thrive. Maryland and Virginia also produced rice and indigo, and the Deep South states of Mississippi, Alabama, and Tennessee produced sugar as a crop. Thus, the southern economy could absorb thousands of slaves each year into the plantation system.

In 1806, President Jefferson asked Congress to consider abolishing the African slave trade. A long debate ensued, but an act, effective January 1, 1808, finally closed the United States to the importation of slaves through the European slave trade. The trading of slaves between states where slaveowners had established colonies of slaves (and sold them like cattle) was banned January 1, 1862 (Kletzing and Crogman 1903). The formal abolishment of slavery was implemented through the Emancipation Proclamation, which President Lincoln signed on January 1, 1863, and which freed about three-fourths of the slaves. The final abolition of slavery came with the passage of the Thirteenth Amendment to the U.S. Constitution in 1865.

As noted, when Africans were brought to the New World they brought their indigenous social patterns and drinking styles with them. North Carolina slaves practiced an activity called "John Canoeing," which closely resembled traditional African rituals—the slaves wore ceremonial costumes and masks while they drank, begged pennies, and danced to tambourine music (Johnson 1937). The persimmon beer parties observed among Virginia slaves (Smith 1838), and the ceremonies for sugarcane cutting that were practiced among Louisiana slaves, closely resembled African harvest rituals (Stampp 1961). Harriet Jacobs in her autobiography, *Incidents in the Life of a Slave Girl* (1861), confirms that many plantation celebrations had African roots.

> Every child rises early on Christmas morning to see the
> Johnkannaus. Without them, Christmas would be shorn of its

greatest attraction. They consist of companies of slaves from the plantations, generally of the lower class. Two athletic men, in calico wrappers, have a net thrown over them, covered with all manner of bright-colored stripes. Cow's tails are fastened to their backs, and their heads are decorated with horns. A box, covered with sheepskin, is called the gumbo box. A dozen beat on this, while others strike triangles and jawbones, to which bands of dancers keep time. For a month previous they are composing songs, which are sung on this occasion. These companies, of a hundred each, turn out early in the morning, and are allowed to go round till twelve o'clock, begging for contributions. Not a door is left unvisited where there is the least chance of obtaining a penny or a glass of rum. They do not drink while they are out but carry the rum home in jugs, to have a carousal. (179)

The early European American settlers also used alcoholic beverages such as ales, brews, ciders, and wines made from a variety of grains and fruits for purposes similar to those of African cultures. Colonists used alcohol at the various social events that were a part of colonial life: weddings, parties, funerals, celebrations, ceremonies, house and barn raisings, church raisings, harvest rituals, and work parties for apple paring, maple sugaring, and corn husking (Greene 1942; Rorabaugh 1979; Aaron and Musto 1979). African American slaves participated in these same events and came to adopt the drinking patterns of the European American colonists.

In both European and American communities drinking until one was drunk or even unconscious had developed as a style of drinking behavior. In the United States, whiskey, a distilled product generally made west of the Appalachian Mountains, began to challenge the popularity of New England rum, as it represented a more potent and thus more desirable drink. Many slaves worked for their owners in the production of whiskey and other alcoholic beverages, and some slaves were particularly valued because of their skills in brewing whiskey, beer, or wine, as revealed in interviews conducted by the Federal Writers Project with former slaves. One of these remembered that "Marse (Master) Alec always had plenty of good whiskey because Uncle Willis made it up for him, and it was made just right" (Killion 1973: 11–12).

Slaves were relatively sober when compared as a group to European settlers and American Indians during this period of history (Genovese

1976) because they drank largely when the "master" allowed it to happen. On some plantations the period between Christmas and New Year's was a time of celebration when the entire plantation drank alcohol:

> [On Christmas Day] Marse Alec would call the grown folks to the big house early in the morning and pass around a big pitcher full of whiskey, then he would put a little whiskey in the same pitcher and fill it with sweetened water and give it to us chillun . . . Us had a big time for a whole week and then on New Year's Day us done a little work just to start the year right and us feasted that day on fresh meat, plenty of cake and whiskey. (Killion 1973:12)

However, Jacobs in *Incidents in the Life of a Slave Girl* suggests that the holiday time was very different on other plantations. New Year's Day was "hiring day" in the community in which she lived, and slaves were sent to distant plantations or even sold on the auction block. Children were torn from parents and husbands from wives, often never to see each other again. Any celebration, with or without the use of alcohol, was short-lived (Jacobs 1861).

The social patterns of drinking for African Americans in slavery became strongly characterized by weekend, holiday, and celebration drinking. The realities of slavery, which demanded daily dawn-to-dusk enforced labor, limited drinking mostly to times when agricultural production slowed. African American women during this period appear to have abstained at a higher rate than men who worked in the fields, primarily because of colonial and traditional African social sanctions against female drinking and because of the highly visible role African American women played as the caretakers of the children of slave owners.

Many sources confirm that slave masters permitted and encouraged alcohol use during harvest and agricultural layover times. Former slaves interviewed in the 1930s reported that for two or three weeks "after [the corn] was all shucked, there was a big celebration in store for the slaves. They cooked up washpots full of lamb, kid, pork and beef and had collard greens that were worth looking at. They had water buckets full of whiskey" (Killion 1973: 82). In addition, liquor was used as an incentive and reward for prodigious feats of labor:

> The moonlight cotton pickings was big old times. They give prizes to the ones picking the most cotton. The prizes was apt to be a

quart of whiskey for the man what picked the most and a dress for
the woman what was ahead. (Ibid.: 83)

Some plantations held "frolics," which often included alcohol, at the end
of planting seasons or at harvests. On many plantations the Fourth of
July celebration marked the end of toil for a season.

> On the Fourth a barbecue was cooked; when dinner was ready all
> the hands got their plows and tools, the mules was brought up and
> gear put on them, and then old Uncle Aaron started up a song
> about the crops was laid and rest time had come, and everybody
> grabbed a hoe or something, put it on their shoulder and joined
> the march around and around the table behind Uncle Aaron.
> (Ibid.: 141)

Allowing slaves the use of alcohol on holidays, at crop-laying time, or
even for weekly frolics was no great indulgence on the part of the slave
master. Holiday celebrations were the only real respite for slaves who
worked from the age of ten until they died. These celebration periods
offered African American people a time of rest and a time of healing after
having been sold to other slave owners, whipped and beaten, chased and
bitten by dogs, sexually assaulted by their "masters," and captured and
punished by slave patrollers. Unfortunately these celebrations begun in
the 1700s contributed to the later development of certain destructive
patterns of African American alcohol and drug use. Moreover, Kenneth
M. Stampp in *The Peculiar Institution: Slavery in the Ante-Bellum South*
suggests that alcohol was used much more commonly in the life of the
slave than merely on holidays and special occasions, and for reasons
other than celebration:

> No law, no threat of the master, ever kept liquor out of the hands
> of slaves or stopped the illicit trade between them and "unscrupu-
> lous" whites. Some masters themselves furnished a supply of
> whiskey for holiday occasions, or winked at violations of state
> laws and of their own rules.
>   There was little truth to the abolitionist charge that masters
> gave liquor to their slaves in order to befuddle their minds and
> keep them in bondage. On the other hand, many bondsmen used
> intoxicants for a good deal more than an occasional pleasant
> stimulant, a mere conviviality of festive occasions. They found that
> liquor provided their only satisfactory escape from the indignities,

the frustration, the emptiness, the oppressive boredom of slavery. Hence, when they had the chance, they resorted to places that catered to the Negro trade or found sanctuaries where they could tipple undisturbed. What filled their alcoholic dreams one can only guess, for the dreams at least were theirs alone. (1961: 370–371)

It is clear that alcohol use by slaves depended on the slave's situation, attitude, and opportunity to get the beverage. In some cases, alcohol use was by expectation and mutual agreement (e.g., Christmas and other holiday celebrations), while in other cases the slaves sought out the alcohol.

ALCOHOL AND DRUG USE AFTER THE CIVIL WAR

The African American church grew dramatically after the Emancipation Proclamation and had a significant influence on the lives of African American people by promoting abstinence and moderate drinking patterns. Revivals, midweek prayer meetings, area conferences, and Sunday church gatherings were central to the lives of most African American people, the majority of whom lived in rural communities, where the church, not the tavern, was the center of community life, the place where the social and educational events of the community were held. The post–Civil War period was also the time when the development of African American higher education occurred—Howard University, Wilberforce University, Morehouse College, Spelman College, Fisk University, Tuskegee University, and other colleges and universities for African Americans opened. Many African Americans were now allowed schooling previously denied them, and work, study, and bettering their lives became their new agenda.

For a short time some African American communities were involved in the Reconstruction movement, which allowed for representation in Congress, voting rights, and funding for schools and agricultural education. However, the Reconstruction period was to be short-lived, for white southerners fully intended to keep African American people in some form of economic and political subjugation. The southern United States increasingly became a place from which African Americans wanted to flee.

In both southern and northern cities during the slavery period, free African Americans had become a substantial presence. However, the end of slavery stimulated the beginning of a rapid increase in migration north, as well as rapid growth in African American populations in southern cities. This increasing urbanization was to change African American patterns of occasional alcohol use into patterns of addiction. Once generally limited to celebrations, weddings, and holidays, alcohol began to be used more widely as a medication to treat the emotional suffering brought on by racism, poverty, and hopelessness, as slaves had used it to treat the emotional suffering of slavery.

As African American urban society developed, the domination and power of the church decreased while the influence and power of the marketplace increased. African American men and women, who could seldom find profitable employment in a rigidly segregated society, increasingly turned to alcohol and drug sales as a source of income.

In American society as a whole the use of nonalcoholic drugs increased. In 1856 the hypodermic syringe was introduced in the United States and during the Civil War was widely used to inject morphine, the primary active ingredient in opium, to relieve the pain of wounded and infected soldiers. So many soldiers became addicted to morphine that they were said to be suffering from "soldier's disease" or the "army disease." Pure cocaine became available at about this same time and was thought to be a cure for morphine addiction, a misconception that led to a cycle of multiple and successive drug use. In the years following the Civil War, soldiers often became addicted to the camphor and opium balls used to treat dysentery, and many soldiers and sailors became easy targets for drug peddlers because of addictions to morphine, opium, cocaine, and hashish they developed while in military service (Ray and Ksir 1990).

Opium use in the United States also grew rapidly as the country imported labor forces from other lands. Chinese workers were brought to the western United States to help build the expanding railroads, and many of them brought with them the habit of smoking opium, which had been stimulated by the legalization of opium in China following the victory of the British in the Opium Wars. Opium, which was brought into China from India by British merchants, appears to have been brought into the United States in this period from the Middle East, as well as from other countries where its production had been encouraged by the British engaged in the opium trade. The number of opium smokers grew quickly in the United States.

In the late 1800s and early 1900s, many physicians regularly prescribed opium and its alkaloids, particularly sulfate of morphine, for ailments such as headaches, sore eyes, toothaches, sore throat, laryngitis, diphtheria, bronchitis, congestion, pneumonia, consumption, gastritis, liver complaints, gallstones, peritonitis, kidney trouble, neuralgia, and rheumatism. Opium and morphine addiction from 1860 to 1900 appears to have been concentrated among women, soldiers, artists, musicians, and physicians (Morgan 1974). African Americans as a group were underrepresented in the growing number of addicts.

At first the Chinese were the racial objects of the antidrug crusades of the late 1800s. In 1875, San Francisco passed the first ordinance in America forbidding opium smoking under severe penalties. New York State passed a similar ordinance in 1882, aimed at opium use in New York City's expanding Chinatown (Kane 1882). A federal act with racist overtones passed in 1890: It allowed only American citizens to import opium or to manufacture smoking opium in the United States. As more laws were passed outlawing the smoking of opium, the price of black-market opium increased. Lower-income addicts began using morphine or heroin, which were both inexpensive and readily available.

By the turn of the century many believed that African Americans had taken up drug use at alarming levels.

> Some of the negro labor camps in the South simply breed addicts. They are deplorable places, as I can testify from observation. The men work about four days in the week and "celebrate" the rest of the time, usually by taking a trip to another camp, where high carnival is held—carnival which involves the use of considerable cocaine or other narcotics when they can be obtained. The supply is usually irregular, and hence there is more of drug debauchery than of regular addiction; but the participants become regular addicts if they leave the camp and take up city residence. (Morgan 1974: 72)

In fact, drug abuse was spreading throughout the entire nation. Gang labor forces at seaport cities such as Baltimore and New Orleans came into contact with drugs as vessels transported larger quantities of opiates into the United States. Traffic on the Great Lakes brought narcotics from Canada into Detroit, Buffalo, Chicago, and Cleveland (Morgan 1974).

At the beginning of the twentieth century, many popular drinks, wine mixtures, and medications included cocaine, opium, and morphine. In 1906 the Pure Food and Drug Act was passed, requiring druggists and patent medicine vendors to specify on the label the amount of habit-forming drugs used in compounds. The act attempted to regulate the use of narcotics in food, drinks, and medicine, and its passage was an important milestone in protecting the health of the nation.

In response to alarming levels of opiate-based drug use, the United States also requested an international conference to discuss controls on the opium trade. Representatives of the United States, Great Britain, and Germany met at The Hague in 1912. For several centuries the British merchants had had a monopoly on opium, which Chinese smugglers took into China for them (Kramer 1979). In 1839 the emperor of China tried to suppress opium smuggling. Pressures mounted, though, and an incident in which drunken British and American soldiers were involved in the killing of a Chinese precipitated the Opium War. The British army and the royal navy won the war, and the smuggling continued. Despite another Opium War in the 1850s, imports of illegal opium continued until 1908, when China and Great Britain finally agreed to limit them. Faced with giving up a very profitable business, Great Britain wanted to enact similar controls over the trade of morphine and cocaine, two drugs manufactured in Germany that were replacing opium. The United States, Great Britain, and Germany finally agreed to control international trade and domestic sale and use of these drugs (Latimer and Goldberg 1981). The Chinese opium trade officially ended in 1913.

In response to the Hague conference, the Harrison Narcotics Act of 1914 was passed. It was titled "*An Act to provide for the registration of, with collectors of internal revenue, and to impose a special tax upon all persons who produce, import, manufacture, compound, deal in, dispense, or give away opium or coca leaves, their salts, derivatives, or preparations, and for other purposes.*"

The Harrison Act put habit-forming drugs under federal control, closed the drug stores that were dispensing addictive drugs, and for a time forced the sellers of these drugs underground. Soon after the law was passed, however, the drug traffic resumed but under extremely different circumstances. The price of heroin and other habit-forming drugs rose dramatically, leading to increased adulteration of the drugs. Addicts who once could procure their supply of drugs at drug stores and through pharmacists were now forced to use illegal means of getting drugs, or were forced to seek treatment as a result of being arrested for violation of the new law. Increasingly African Americans began to be numbered among those selling as well as using opium, heroin, and morphine.

While the United States was busy passing an antinarcotic act it was also heading toward prohibition of alcohol, a move that challenged the long-standing acceptance of alcohol as having a positive role in society, both socially and medicinally (even sick children were quieted and thought to be cured by small sips of alcoholic drinks). In fact, early on hard drinking had become associated with hard work through the use of alcohol at house raisings, harvesting celebrations, husking, quilting, logrolling, and all of the major festivities (Sinclair 1962). Traditionally, alcohol was supplied to soldiers and sailors. During the War of Independence in 1776, each soldier at Valley Forge received an official daily ration of a half pint of whiskey, depending on the supply that the quartermaster had available (Sinclair 1962). In 1811, Dr. Benjamin Rush, who had been physician-general of the Middle Department of the Continental Army, cautioned against the use of liquor and issued a famous pamphlet advocating complete abstinence. He was a tremendous influence on the preacher Lyman Beecher, who in the early 1830s appealed to God's law as well as increasing medical knowledge to promote the cause of prohibition. Across the nation, large numbers of people joined together to express their concerns about the use of alcohol, the liquor traffic, and the negative influence of the liquor industry in the United States. Ultimately the growth of these religious and social movements resulted in the formation of the United States Temperance Union in 1836.

The temperance movement was rooted in nationalism—a belief that self-control was essential for the country, that abstinence would bring social reform, that the movement against saloons and drinking would eliminate prostitution and crime. However, in the South the movement was affected by the racist belief that Prohibition was needed as a means of preventing interracial sex.

In the North, African Americans joined the movement in significant numbers. They founded such groups as the Colored American Temperance Society in Philadelphia in the early 1830s, the New England Temperance Society of Colored People in 1836, the Connecticut State Temperance Society of Colored People, and the African Temperance Society in New York in the early 1840s.

This major reform movement grew into strong prohibition movements in twelve states, until the Civil War put a temporary damper on the movement. Although thirteen states passed prohibition laws between 1851 and 1855, nine had repealed them by 1868, under extreme pressure from the liquor industry. The National Prohibition Party, organized in 1874, started a new movement for the prohibition of alcohol. Much of the party's focus was on the link between alcohol use, race, and crime (especially sexual crimes). Over a period of almost fifty years various groups worked for national prohibition. By 1920 there was enough national support to pass the Eighteenth Amendment against the sale or transport of alcohol within the United States.

The amendment gained the uncertain support of a nation involved in the suffering of World War I. Once the war was over, however, it became clear that national support for the movement was real. The Methodist and Baptist churches and fundamentalist sects formed the core support for Prohibition in the South. Not only did "this dominant village middle class [provide] religious fodder for pulpit politics and prohibition," it "gave the Ku Klux Klan the majority of its four million members during its revival after the Great War" (Sinclair 1962: 18).

White southerners used the Prohibition movement to promulgate their prejudices against and fears of African American males. They spread the rumor that liquor sometimes gave the African American man, stimulated by the pictures of seminaked women on the labels of whiskey bottles, the courage to overcome his inferior status and to loose his sexual desires on white women (Irwin 1908). They believed African American men should be prohibited from drinking liquor, and, to a lesser degree, it was agreed that white men should be included in this prohibition. Since African Americans were segregated from white society and discriminatory laws denied or restricted their right to vote, it seemed equally appropriate to the white population to deny the African American the right to drink liquor.

In the early 1900s and following World War I, African Americans migrated in large numbers from the rural South to the urban centers of the North, seeking employment opportunities and hoping to escape from the rural poverty, repression, violence, and racial segregation of the South (Gwinnell 1928). For a good many African Americans, the Great Migration (discussed in Chapter 2) changed their pattern of alcohol use as well as their location. The urban milieu, where social activities took place in taverns and clubs, fostered regular and excessive drinking, rather than drinking to celebrate special occasions. In Chicago, New York, Philadelphia, and Boston, African American communities increasingly became the place where whites practiced their vices. During the Prohibition era, many African American clubs and stores sold illegal whiskey, and law enforcement officials often ignored alcohol and other drug sales in these communities. Whites came to African American communities to hear African American music, to party, to patronize houses of prostitution, and to gamble.

African Americans became a prime target for the illegal alcohol sales of white liquor traders (Drake and Cayton 1945; McKay 1968). As segregation and discrimination kept most African American men in the North out of higher education and lucrative jobs, a small number profited from the illegal liquor trade. This pattern of promoting illegal substances in African American communities was repeated with the mass marketing and distribution of heroin, the use of which reached epidemic proportions.

Illegal drug use in the early 1900s was limited to subcultures within the larger African American community. For example, African American men fighting in World War I were exposed to drug use in the port cities of Europe and North Africa, but when they returned home they usually did not continue their drug experimentation. The majority of African American families were involved in a struggle against segregation, poverty, and racial violence, and drug use was generally not a paramount concern.

In the 1920s and 1930s, however, African American businesses began to take advantage of the desire of the populace to escape from both poverty and sobriety. In the large cities of the United States, African American communities became places to escape from the rigid racial and social boundaries of the nation. Jazz and dance clubs, houses of prostitution, gambling houses, and after-hours clubs became an emerging part of African American society. These clubs also provided a haven where those African American church members who wanted to could find an escape from the more rigid teachings of African American preachers.

In the 1930s statistics began to indicate that large numbers of African Americans were known narcotics addicts, chiefly because they were disproportionately represented in the known addict populations of major urban areas. According to a report on opium addiction in Chicago from 1928 to 1934, African Americans represented only 6.9 percent of the population but made up 17.3 percent of the addict population (Dai 1937). Across the United States in Los Angeles, San Francisco, Seattle, Chicago, New York, Philadelphia, Miami, Pittsburgh, and Detroit, African American addiction of various kinds was growing, a growth that had a multiplicity of causes. As America came out of the Depression,

African Americans became more prosperous because of their work in automotive factories. Prohibition was to end soon, and all of America would be involved in mobilizing for World War II.

African American night life—and alcohol and drug use—continued to expand during the war. In geographically isolated Seattle, over thirty-four jazz-oriented clubs prospered during this period. There were clubs with full casinos, gentleman pimps in the bars, and heroin and cocaine for sale (de Barros 1993).

African Americans who fought in World War II distinguished themselves in combat, although the armed forces were segregated until 1948. The war brought new prosperity to African American soldiers and factory and shipyard workers and also provided African American males with the freedom of travel. Treated with respect and equality in France and other nations, few were prepared to return to the racism and limited opportunity of the United States.

2 THE PAST
FIFTY YEARS

With the return of both white and African American drug-using soldiers from Vietnam, the entire country became a fertile field for the growth of heroin use.

In the late 1940s, heroin, in good supply and inexpensive, was used more and more in large urban African American communities as the northern migration of African Americans from the southern states continued and newly discharged veterans settled in places like Los Angeles, Oakland, Seattle, New Jersey, Pittsburgh, Kansas City, Cleveland, and Detroit. Many returning African American veterans had taken pain-relief drugs during World War II and were addicted to opiates. Initially, a dollar would buy enough for a good high for several people and $2.00-per-day habits were common. As demand increased, so did the price—and the mixing of other substances with heroin (adulteration) became more frequent. The use of alcohol-based cough syrups and prescription drugs like Darvon and Ritalin, as well as various barbiturates and amphetamines, was on the upswing and in the 1950s and the 1960s marijuana was more often the drug favored by musicians and in social situations. Previously, marijuana use had been largely restricted to specific subculture groups, including prisoners, ex-prisoners, pimps, prostitutes, and military personnel. Now it was being used at middle-class parties and in middle-class African American communities. Particularly on the East Coast, it was available at a very low cost to younger people, and it was shared among different cultural and racial groups. Studies showed that narcotics addiction at this time affected males more than females and that African American males in their twenties used various combinations of alcohol, marijuana, psychedelic drugs, stimulants, sedatives, heroin, and other opiates (O'Donnell et al. 1976).

While heroin addiction, concentrated in urban areas, constituted the largest drug problem in African American communities during this period, its actual impact was small when compared with the effects of alcohol on African American rural and urban populations. The traditional African American community was in denial about the level of alcoholism, and this resulted in a serious health problem. It was almost as if communities accepted high levels of alcohol use as a part of being African American in an oppressive and racist nation. In *Alcoholism and the Urban Negro Population*, which discusses patterns of urban African American male addiction, Peter Bourne argued that the emotional and mental state of many African American individuals in urban America creates an attitude where almost any pleasure is better than the current reality. He advanced the idea that drugs offer an accessible and immediate pleasure not to be denied or deferred by the individual who believes that future opportunities are limited and who is discouraged about the prospects for a job, more income, job promotion, and a more pleasurable or meaningful existence. Bourne suggests that this discouragement and depression leads to seeking immediate pleasure from drugs and other sources.

Treatment opportunities outside of public hospitals were limited during the 1950s and 1960s; public programs tended to be oriented toward middle-class white alcoholics. Community-based programs were just starting, and Alcoholics Anonymous had not yet extended its programs into the majority of African American communities. Some economic development programs produced by the War on Poverty included treatment programs for alcohol and other drug abuse, and programs funded by the Office of Economic Opportunity in Atlanta and by Harlem Hospital in New York City were examples of a growing trend toward community-based agencies.

Low-income African American rural males, including former agricultural laborers whose jobs had been replaced by machines, repre-

Big Knocker
it shot

BON APPÉTIT

America's Food and Entertaining Magazine

12 issues just $14.97

4D27

Save 58%!

Name _____

(please print)

Address _____ Apt. _____

City _____ State _____ Zip _____

☐ Payment enclosed ☐ Bill me later

In Canada, Bon Appétit is $30 including GST. Your first issue mails within 6 weeks.

sented a particularly difficult population to reach. The despairing and alcoholic marginalized African American laborer of the 1960s evokes images of the despairing unemployed crack addicts of the 1990s, standing on the street corners of our cities.

The African American church in the 1960s was at its peak as an advocate of African American liberation and freedom. The church organized its African American members as well as surrounding communities in the most effective struggle for justice and equality America had ever seen. However, in the cities of Chicago, New York, Boston, Cleveland, San Francisco, Los Angeles, and Washington, D.C., another kind of movement was taking place—the beginning of a slow but steadily growing heroin epidemic. Few African American churches in these cities recognized or acknowledged the epidemic as a threat to African American liberation and freedom.

In Harlem, the heroin epidemic was portrayed as an addiction of artists, musicians, and individuals on the fringes of society. The real victims of the heroin epidemic in New York and other cities were several generations of African American and Puerto Rican youth. The New York Urban League, Young Life Campaign, Harlem Hospital, many community clinics, and several New York African American Presbyterian and Baptist churches made heroic efforts to confront the drug epidemic. They unfortunately lacked the financial stability and the understanding of addiction needed to mount an effective campaign against it.

Drug syndicates gained control of drug production and distribution in the 1950s and 1960s and continue this control today. Younger African Americans gained expertise in drug preparation, packaging, and sales, and a new class of criminal in African American society was born: the drug dealers. Addiction in African American communities became intergenerational, with entire families involved with drug use and drug sales.

THE VIETNAM WAR

From the mid-1960s to the early 1970s the U.S. government deepened its involvement in the Vietnam conflict. African Americans served in large numbers and again with distinction. By the end of the war it was estimated that 25 percent of the American forces in Southeast Asia had been African American and that many of these soldiers were addicted to heroin. The Vietnam experience exposed thousands of rural and urban African American youth to a violent and often meaningless war that left deep scars of guilt, anger, and pain.

Wallace Terry (1984) shares an oral history of twenty African American soldiers who served in Vietnam. One of the soldiers, Specialist 4 Richard J. Ford III, stated, "People that wasn't even there tell us the war was worthless. That a man lost his life following orders. It was worthless, they be saying. . . . I feel used. I feel manipulated. I feel violated" (52).

The pattern of drug use in African American communities between 1965 and 1980 was seriously affected by the Vietnam War. Drugs were used by the soldiers in Vietnam to numb the horror of seeing friends maimed or killed. The use of opium, heroin, morphine, and marijuana was both tolerated and ignored by a military that was more interested in a steady supply of fighting soldiers than in their sobriety and emotional health. Richard Kunnes (1972) suggested that the U.S. Army tolerated marijuana use in Vietnam from 1963 to 1968, but, as more newspaper accounts reported its use, the government began a campaign to eradicate the practice among American soldiers.

> It was a very efficient campaign. Marijuana is bulky and the smoke is detectable by smell. In one week there were thousands of arrests for possession of marijuana. Much official satisfaction was expressed in press releases which indicated that the drug problem in Vietnam was being brought under control. Not surprisingly many soldiers simply switched to a stronger, more available, less detectable, cheap drug—heroin. (150)

Kunnes indicated that over sixteen treatment programs were in place in Vietnam at the height of war activity in 1971. In barrack sweeps called Operation Golden Flow, many enlisted men were found to be "opiate positive." Heroin and opiate users identified in this process were promised amnesty if they took part in Army-sponsored treatment programs, but the stigma of drug involvement and reduced opportunity for promotion and security clearances made promises of amnesty empty and unpersuasive. Soldiers who tested positive were separated from their units and placed in the Sixth Convalescent Center at Cam Rahn Bay or T. C. Hill in Lon Binh. All soldiers had the right to appeal their confinement, but in actual practice it was the officers and well-connected individuals who were not forced into treatment. Kunnes describes the success of appeals: "such appeals were unlikely for the average soldier, particularly if he is black or considered radical by Army standards" (1972: 166). Discharges from the Armed Services for drug abuse rose sharply at the height of American involvement in Vietnam.

Vietnam veterans, returning to brothers, sisters, and their extended families, influenced a new wave of addiction in African American communities. Up to this point, heroin use had been mainly limited to the urban areas. With the return of both white and African American drug-using soldiers from Vietnam, the entire country became a fertile field for the growth of heroin use.

CASE STUDY
Mr. A.

Mr. A., an African American veteran, was fifty-four years old at the time of this interview. He was born on a farm near Houston, Texas, and is the oldest of three children.

As a young boy he saw that drinking was socially acceptable on Fridays and Saturdays, even for his very religious family, who went to church every Sunday. "Home brew" made in the woods was available for family members, and as a young boy he was allowed to "drink a little bit" of beer and whiskey.

As a young African American, Mr. A. said that he experienced two different childhoods, one in the city and one in the country. He chopped wood, picked cotton, loaded hay, and did other field work with members of his family during the 1950s in Texas, which was racially segregated. When it was not cotton-picking time, he lived with his grandmother and attended school in the city. He also added that the truant officer would be looking for him if he was absent from school.

Because little opportunity existed for him in the segregated South, Mr. A. took the same route as many other African American males and joined the Army as soon as he finished high school. He was assigned to duty in Korea in the early 1960s and to Vietnam in the mid-1960s. African Americans comprised about 25 percent of his company. Although the military had been integrated, there was still separation. African Americans were primarily foot soldiers, while whites were mainly in the officer ranks.

Mr. A. said that the army "villages" or base camps were

segregated: African American and white soldiers lived in separate villages with their particular music, drugs, and women. Mr. A. indicated that since food, housing, and clothing were provided, their soldiers' pay was spent on having a good time. In order to deal with the feelings of isolation and alienation resulting from racism within Army units, Mr. A. said that the African American soldiers developed special handshakes and ways of greeting each other as "bloods." White officers observing these behaviors became suspicious, and the gulf between racial groups widened.

Mr. A. found that opium was readily available in Korea, and he became addicted when he was nineteen years old. He smoked the opium, and his supply came through native Korean merchants. Mr. A. said that Army officials appeared to tolerate drug use among the troops as long as it was done while off duty. Mr. A. reported falling asleep once while on duty because of his drug use, and his superior officer was unable to wake him. As a result of this incident he was reduced in rank but was allowed to stay in the military. While returning to the United States by ship from Korea, he went through withdrawal from opium, and the pain and sickness of the withdrawal convinced him that opiate drugs "were not for him."

Mr. A. went on to serve in Vietnam in the mid-1960s as a noncommissioned officer in the First Air Mobile Unit, or "sky troopers." The sky troopers moved troops and assisted the ground soldiers in destroying enemy villages. Mr. A. saw that alcohol, marijuana, opium, and cocaine were available and used by soldiers in Vietnam. Many African American soldiers were put in Lon Bien Jail, or LBJ, for drug-related problems.

Mr. A. had kicked his opium addiction, but while in Vietnam he drank a bottle of "good whiskey" every day. The soldiers below him in rank were not able to get good whiskey and drank cheap "rot gut" booze. He believes that drug use was confined to base camp and was not resorted to "in the bush" where the war was being fought and where lives were at stake.

Mr. A. is currently working with African American males who are veterans of military service and who developed addictions to cocaine, heroin, alcohol, and other drugs. He says that most of them use drugs to "numb the pain." According to Mr. A., many of the African American soldiers "busted" for drug use in Vietnam opted

to take "administrative discharges" in order to avoid going to jail.
This discharge is less than an honorable discharge and affected their
ability to secure employment upon returning to the United States.

Mr. A. indicated that African American Vietnam veterans re-
turning to the United States ETS (end of term of service) were
dropped off at one of two discharge centers, Fort Lewis, Washing-
ton, or Oakland, California. These veterans returned to a country
consumed by racial strife and violence in the major urban areas and
did not receive the customary welcome extended to soldiers who
had put their lives on the line for their country. Mr. A. feels that
African Americans from families in the South fared somewhat bet-
ter than those from families in the North. In his opinion, the north-
ern families tended to turn their backs on the returning soldiers and
to accuse them of abandoning their communities and "fighting the
wrong enemy" by going off to an undeclared war in Southeast Asia.
Although Mr. A. was able to secure employment after returning
from the Vietnam War, he continued to be addicted to alcohol and
drank whiskey on a daily basis until he decided to seek treatment.

RACIAL INTEGRATION

In addition to the influence of the Vietnam War during the 1960s and
1970s, the increasing integration of American society also changed the
patterns of drug use among African Americans. Contact with the
counterculture or so-called hippie community led African Americans to
experiment with mescaline, LSD, PCP, and other hallucinogenic drugs
not previously introduced into African American culture. While these
drugs did not necessarily cause ongoing addictions on a widespread basis, they did cause short-term and, in some cases, long-term disabilities.

Communities and races that would not speak to each other in the
1950s were going to school, dating, drinking, and smoking marijuana
with each other in the 1960s and 1970s. Until this time, epidemic drug
use had been largely limited to urban communities. The growing leftist
political movements characterized by groups such as the Students for a
Democratic Society and the Black Panthers tolerated drug use and exposed middle-class African American college students to addiction.
These students were uneducated about drug addiction and often not
prepared to make healthy choices that included the avoidance of drug

use. Getting along with white college classmates or hanging out with African American fraternity brothers or sorority sisters could mean getting "stoned" every weekend. Some African American college students developed addictions they could not control and ended up dropping out of school.

CASE STUDY
Mr. B.

Mr. B. was born and raised in a small town in Oregon by a high-achieving middle-class family. He was thirty years old at the time of this interview and in treatment for crack cocaine addiction in an outpatient facility. The beginning of his drug addiction can be traced to marijuana use as a college sophomore. Mr. B. was an average student and athlete at a southern predominantly white university. His first two college years were fairly successful. After being introduced to marijuana, he began to smoke daily, and in order to support his drug habit he sold drugs on campus. Mr. B. appears to have little insight into how he moved from college attendance to crack cocaine addiction.

Raised in a completely white school environment and community, Mr. B. feels that "hanging with the brothers" and learning how to participate in African American culture are very important. His desire to belong and to bond with African American brothers and sisters has never been fully realized. Stuck in a pattern of relapse, treatment, rehabilitation, and repeated relapse, Mr. B.'s dream of becoming "educated" and accepted by other African Americans is currently impossible because of his well-developed addiction.

Mr. B. never fully bonds with the treatment recovery group and struggles with authenticity, emotional expression, and honesty. Better educated than most of his recovering peers, he has found that his college experience and middle-class ways seem to limit his recovery because he would rather express his thoughts than his feelings. A deeper examination of his family background reveals a father who may be a controlled alcoholic but who has worked hard to pull his family into middle-class status. Mr. B.'s deepest bond is with drugs, and any freedom from their domination has proved to be temporary so far.

AFRICAN AMERICAN LEADERSHIP

African American community leadership in the late 1960s and early 1970s conceptualized the real enemy as racism, which generated police violence, unemployment, housing discrimination, and lack of opportunities for African Americans. The nature of the African American struggle was identified by moderate African American leadership as a struggle for denied opportunity. Therefore, the political agenda of African American moderates involved opening up legal avenues that improved access to employment, housing, and educational opportunities. More radical African American leadership identified the struggle of African American people as a class struggle against white power. The Black Power movement openly challenged white power and authority.

Both African American moderate and radical leadership envisioned the threat to African American people as external oppression, racism, and violence. More and more, however, the threat to African American liberation came from black-on-black violence, crime, and addiction. African American leaders were ill-prepared to confront danger within the African American community, and as a result they did not mobilize their communities to deal with the initial epidemic of heroin addiction in the 1970s. While many social workers, physicians, and community organizers realistically understood the threat of addiction, national African American religious and political leadership, as before, did not sound any significant alarm about the perils of African American addiction. This reluctance to deal with the earliest warnings of an African American drug epidemic has proved particularly destructive to communities devastated by the wave of crack cocaine addiction in the 1980s and 1990s.

THE CONSOLIDATION OF THE DRUG TRADE

Perhaps the most significant event to affect patterns of African American addiction happened outside the United States in the Latin American country of Chile during the early 1970s. Marxist president Salvador Allende Gossens was overthrown and replaced by Chilean army general Augusto Pinochet Ugarte. By the end of General Pinochet's first year in office, seventy-five drug traffickers were in jail and another twenty bosses had been sent to the United States. Until this time, the cocaine industry had been a cottage industry largely limited to Chile. According to Guy Gugliotta (1989), "The Chileans made a lush living from cocaine, but the market was relatively small" (23).

The cocaine laboratories closed in Chile and moved to Colombia. The coca leaves continued to come in from Bolivia and Peru, and the industry was taken over by older, established Colombian smugglers from Medellín, Bogotá, and Cali. These older smugglers quickly gave way to younger and more aggressive Colombian cocaine traffickers who envisioned sending tons of cocaine into the United States instead of twenty or thirty kilos at a time (a kilo is 2.2 pounds). Names like Escobar, Ochoa, and Lehder began to come up in Drug Enforcement Agency (DEA) intelligence reports, but U.S. authorities were more concerned with marijuana smuggling than cocaine trafficking. They did not foresee the implementation of marijuana smuggling methods and large-scale utilization of cargo ships and airplanes to move cocaine into the United States.

In 1974, a kilo of cocaine could be bought for $2,000 in Colombia and sold for as much as $55,000 in the United States. By 1980, the DEA estimated that the cocaine trade brought $7 billion annually into southern Florida in comparison to the $5-billion annual income provided by tourism. On March 9, 1982, customs inspectors of a TAMPA Airline cargo flight discovered 3,906 pounds of cocaine with a value of $100 million. Large amounts of cocaine were coming into the United States, and much of it was heading directly into African American communities.

By 1983, in Medellín, Colombia, 80 percent of the drug users had switched to a smokeable form of cocaine base called *bazukos* (Gugliotta 1989). This type of cocaine is highly addictive. Soon those who marketed cocaine found a way to chemically transform the cocaine base into a more purified form called "crack." It became the mass-market drug on which the Colombian cartel placed their hopes.

Increasingly, the supplies of ether and acetone necessary for making powder cocaine were being intercepted by Colombian government and DEA officials. For example, DEA officials once placed a small radio transmitter in a chemical barrel bound for Colombia. Once in Colombia, this transmitter broadcast the location of an important laboratory and shipping area for cocaine. The need for ether and acetone made cocaine smugglers highly vulnerable.

Crack proved to be more highly addictive than cocaine powder. By 1985, the urban communities of the United States were in the midst of a crack epidemic, fueled by large shipments from Colombia. By the end of 1985, twenty-five tons of crack cocaine had been seized in South Florida alone. Los Angeles, New York, Miami, and Philadelphia quickly became centers of crack and cocaine distribution. One African American addict interviewed in the summer of 1992 recalled that

> Crack really appeared big in 1985. It first showed up here in 1984 but people lacked real information about it. A lot of people were still selling speed, marijuana, and cough syrups when crack first showed up. Early crack dealing here in Philadelphia was mostly done by Dominicans and Italians. By 1987, African American youth began to move heavily into crack cocaine sales. (Interview conducted with a resident of the Genesis II Treatment facility, Philadelphia)

During the 1970s, the high cost of "powder" cocaine, used intravenously or intranasally, limited its use among African Americans. However, as cocaine began to be smoked through a chemical process called free basing, where baking soda and cocaine were mixed and heated into a smokeable compound, more African Americans began using cocaine to reach the euphoric high that resulted from free basing. Crack cocaine replaced the complex free-basing process. A small, hard, powdery rock substance, crack could be smoked through a small glass stem or in a small pipe, and in two or three years became the drug of choice, other than alcohol, for many African American drug users. A single "hit" could be purchased for just a few dollars.

Until the epidemic of crack cocaine hit the African American community, the majority of drugs used had a "ceiling" of use: a large amount of alcohol, marijuana, or heroin induces a relaxed state followed by low-level activity or sleep. Crack cocaine, however, after only a few minutes produces an intense but brief euphoria, and the user then goes on a desperate search for more of the drug. In a few hours, a person could spend an entire paycheck and still go looking for more money for drugs. In a few months, the crack cocaine addict can experience the type of financial loss and emotional breakdown that alcoholism produces over years. For those individuals coming from families where addiction is an ongoing family illness, crack cocaine addiction appears to progress even faster. In such cases, the loss of control over the drug and one's resources comes so quickly that the addict is caught completely off guard.

AFRICAN AMERICAN GANGS AND
CRACK COCAINE DISTRIBUTION

Because of the demand for large and regular amounts of crack cocaine to supply the growing number of habits, new patterns of distribution and marketing developed in African American communities. The involvement of African American gangs in crack distribution and sales became the largest new factor. Drug sales were limited to certain gangs, who each claimed a certain territory, and the twenty-four-hour "rock house" emerged as the place where one could get and smoke crack cocaine, sell stolen property for drugs, find sexual pleasure, and stay off the street as long as one had money.

Gangs such as the Crips and Bloods started out in California but quickly spread throughout the United States. Due to legal prosecution in Los Angeles in 1986 and 1987, many gang members fled that city for San Francisco, Sacramento, Portland, Tacoma, and Seattle, as well as many other cities across the United States. The smaller West coast cities were no more prepared for these African American youth gangs than the Drug Enforcement Administration had been prepared for the Colombians' entrance into cocaine trafficking. Moving to the poorest of African American communities, these gang members quickly organized gang sets (local affiliates) among their peers in housing projects.

By 1988, crack cocaine had firmly embedded itself in the fabric of African American life. Rival drug-trafficking gangs have subjected major urban areas to violence on playgrounds, in stores, and in homes. The crack cocaine epidemic has left everyone wondering, "What is happening to our communities?" It slowed, for a time, only when foreign or midlevel suppliers temporarily experienced a low supply of the drug.

THE CRACK COCAINE EPIDEMIC CONTINUES

In early 1991, interdiction efforts and police action reduced the amount of cocaine available for street use, but the amounts of money involved as well as the rapidly increasing supply of crack cocaine hampered the long-term effectiveness of law enforcement. Seemingly, there are simply too many people selling the drug and too many suppliers importing the drug for law enforcement officials to make any lasting difference.

One of the most reliable sources of information regarding inner-city addiction in the United States comes from the Department of Justice

Drug Use Forecasting (DUF) reports. While many government agencies have released politically motivated statistics that testify to dropping cocaine rates in the United States, the DUF reports have captured the patterns of addiction for inner-city offender populations with a greater reliability. DUF reports are based on samples of quarterly urinalyses in county jails across twenty-three American cities. Reading these quarterly reports over the past few years allows one to track the movement of the crack epidemic through cities like Washington, D.C., Philadelphia, New York City, Los Angeles, and Atlanta.

Cocaine use in the major northern cities has increased steadily since 1985. DUF reports showed cocaine-positive tests of arrested Philadelphia males in 1988 to be as high as 72 percent. The rates for males in New York City were 74 percent, Miami 64 percent, and Los Angeles 60 percent. Female arrestees in Detroit were found to be cocaine positive in 71 percent of the population, in Chicago females were 70 percent positive for cocaine, and in New York City 75 percent were positive (U.S. Department of Justice 1990).

The most recent statistics available on inner-city cocaine use in offender populations are for the second quarter of 1993. In New York City males were positive for cocaine at a rate of 64 percent, in Philadelphia at a rate of 56 percent, in Chicago 53 percent, and in Birmingham 51 percent. In Atlanta, Miami, Houston, and New Orleans, rates ranged from 41 to 61 percent (U.S. Department of Justice 1993).

The crack cocaine epidemic has also contributed to an increase in heroin and alcohol use in the African American community. As a result of the restlessness, alertness, and acute paranoia caused by the use of crack cocaine, many users "come off" of a run of crack use by drinking one to three forty-ounce bottles of beer or by using some other depressant drug. Often when slowing or stopping the crack cocaine habit, an individual is left with a strong addiction to alcohol.

In communities where heroin is widely available, it also is used to come down from the crack cocaine high. There has been a steady rise in some cities in the practices of injecting heroin and cocaine together in a form called a "speedball" and of smoking cocaine and heroin together in the form of a "brown rock" (New York Drug Research Harlem Street Observation Unit, Interview, Summer 1992). Much of the increase in heroin use may be attributed to the popularity of these practices, and the use of needles puts addicts at serious risk for HIV/AIDS.

Opiate use among offenders in cities with majority African American populations was highest in the second quarter of 1991 in Manhattan and Chicago, at 23 percent and 16 percent, respectively. Compared to crack use, opiate use in offender populations in the largest northern cities is about 30 percent. Among female and male offenders testing positive for opiates, 85 percent of males and 87 percent of females tested positive for cocaine. Opiate prevention and treatment must focus on cocaine treatment and prevention as well. Current research on crack populations suggests that the intensity of the crack cocaine high almost always leads to individuals replacing marijuana use with crack use. Drug histories taken from over fifty crack-addicted African American males involved in a study in Seattle, Washington, illustrate how once crack is smoked, marijuana use becomes almost negligible. It is interesting to note that in 1991 the highest measurements of marijuana-positive tests occurred in Portland (42 percent), San Diego (38 percent), Indianapolis (38 percent), and Fort Lauderdale (35 percent), the cities with the highest white populations. Cities with larger African American populations report much lower levels of marijuana use: Atlanta at 14 percent, New York at 18 percent, Washington, D.C., at 10 percent, and Chicago at 33 percent (ibid.).

In the 1990s, increased drug use and dealing throughout American society continues to be tolerated and is rampant in many African American communities. Traditional African American institutions such as churches and black colleges, fraternities, and sororities are still not prepared to deal with their members or students who use drugs. These institutions tend to ignore drug use, especially if using drugs does not cause open conflict or difficulty. Many leaders in the African American community continue to see racism, discrimination, and lack of employment opportunities as the major problems, and the feeling remains widespread that the use of drugs for social and recreational purposes is largely an individual choice.

3 ALCOHOL

And be not drunk with wine, wherein is excess;
but be filled with the spirit.

—Ephesians 5:10

Alcoholism has been a problem for many centuries and emerged as a major problem for Americans, particularly African Americans, in the 1900s. The present epidemic of alcohol abuse in African American communities is directly related to the contemporary use of drugs in American culture. In order to understand the nature of the alcohol problem and its impact on the African American community, it is necessary to review the factors that have led to pain, denial, depression, and alcohol abuse by individuals and families in these communities. We must attempt to understand what constitutes the alcohol abuse problem in the African American community, and what are the key factors that influence drug use.

African Americans, a genetic and cultural mix of African, European, American Indian, Latino, and Asian heritage, are the nation's largest racial minority group, totaling 27 million people and making up 12 percent of the U.S. population. African Americans in the United States represent considerable cultural diversity: urban African Americans from the West Indies have a unique cultural experience and do not share the same background with African Americans from rural Mississippi or Latin America. Middle-class African Americans and working-class African Americans have different economic experiences that lead to a further differentiation of cultural experiences. However, despite this diversity, there are certain historical factors (such as slavery, racism, discrimination, prejudice) and physical factors (hair texture and other physical attributes) that are so predominant that they affect the African American experience as a whole. This chapter discusses historical, social, and cultural factors related to the use of alcohol and presents some theories regarding the reasons that some African Americans become addicted to alcohol.

After the emancipation of slaves, during the early years of the Reconstruction period, the drinking patterns of some African Americans changed dramatically as they celebrated and tested their new freedom by consuming alcohol on a regular basis. Stereotypes emerged of African Americans as people who drank to excess and were lazy or dangerous when drinking. However, the majority of African Americans reflected the attitudes, values, and beliefs of the New England missionaries and Freedman's Bureau officials who traveled to the South to assist the former slaves. These individuals modeled puritanical and moralistic views of drinking behavior for African Americans. Many African Americans supported and promoted abstinence and temperance through the church and the "colored" temperance movement (Meir 1964; Sellers 1943; Whitener 1945).

The advocates of the temperance movement considered any drinking of alcohol to be a sign of irresponsible behavior and believed that abstinence was the appropriate rule for behaving responsibly. In many cases, European Americans in the movement believed that the major challenge in dealing with the overall drinking problems of the entire South was controlling drinking by African Americans. However, through the end of the nineteenth century, African American problems with alcohol appeared to be minimal. This is supported by the 1880 U.S. mortality statistics reported on alcoholism:

> [T]he proportion in those parts of the country in which the color
> distinction is made is much greater among whites than among
> the colored, the figures being for the Irish 6.7, for the Germans
> 2.7, for the whites 2.5, and for the colored 0.7 per 1,000 deaths
> from known causes. A large proportion of the deaths reported due
> to alcoholism occur in connection with delirium tremens, and this
> form of disease is rare in the colored race. (U.S. Census Office 1886:
> lxvii)

In the early twentieth century, African American participation in the temperance movement declined, both generally and in terms of African American temperance societies, because the southern temperance movement had become racist and supported white supremacy, Jim Crow laws, and the notion that African Americans were sexually depraved and violent. Most African American leaders withdrew from the movement and began to focus more on social and political equality (Herd 1983).

THE GREAT MIGRATION TO THE NORTH

The Great Migration of African Americans from the South to the urban North, which began in the 1900s and has continued into the present decade, was going strong in the mid-thirties, when Jimmy Rushing and Count Basie wrote the song "Going to Chicago":

> Going to Chicago
> Sorry but I can't take you
> Well, I'm going to Chicago
> Sorry but I can't take you
> There's nothing in Chicago
> for a monkey woman to do.

It was the promise of a better life, greater economic opportunity, and freedom from racial oppression in the South that led to the massive migration of rural African Americans to the North. The Twelfth Census of the United States in 1900 indicated that about 80 percent of the African American (Negro) population lived in the South, and the Thirteenth Census of 1910 indicated an increase to 89 percent. However, as a result of the mass migration to the North, by the Fifteenth Census of 1930 the number of African Americans living in the South had decreased to 79 percent. At the same time, the number of African Americans living in urban centers (in the North and in the South) rose rapidly, as indicated by the increase from 34 percent in 1920 (Fourteenth Census) to 49 percent in 1940 (Sixteenth Census). By 1960 the percentage of African Americans living in the South had decreased to 60 percent (Eighteenth Census). This migration out of the South has continued—only 54 percent of the African American population lived in the South in 1990 (Twenty-first Census).

The major urban centers that were the focus of this migration in the early 1900s were New York, Detroit, Chicago, and Cleveland. Thousands of African American people moved from rural communities in the South dominated by church life and agricultural production to urban communities in the North, where jazz clubs, taverns, and social life flourished. These individuals and families were faced with the daunting task of adapting to a fundamentally different environment. Research has indicated that a social migration and dislocation of this magnitude results in tremendous stress on individuals and families and severely challenges cultural norms, values, and behaviors.

Throughout the Great Migration, African Americans continued to use alcohol for holidays and ceremonial occasions, a pattern of weekend drinking and celebrating traceable in part to the use of alcohol by native Africans to mark special occasions such as the end of a work period. However, in the northern reception cities of New York, Detroit, Chicago, and Cleveland, the small row houses and apartments in run-down and segregated neighborhoods were not large enough for the kind of celebrating and festivities that were common in the rural South. As a result of widespread discrimination and oppression, opportunities for entertainment or socializing were severely limited for African Americans, and neighborhood taverns became a main gathering place for drinking, socializing, celebrating, partying, and carrying on political activities in the African American community.

In the 1920s, Prohibition provided many African Americans with the opportunity to become successful bootleggers. Very quickly African American communities in the cities became the focal point for night life and the illegal liquor traffic. Bootlegging, liquor parties, rent parties, and operating speakeasies became a way to make fast money, although most of the alleged financial profit from bootlegging did not remain in the African American community but went to white liquor-traders. Many African Americans became a part of this urban subculture and were involved directly in the illegal bootlegging trade of manufacturing, distributing, and selling alcohol. They reaped financial benefits at a time when segregation and discrimination kept most African Americans out of higher education and lucrative jobs, and their exploits against white law-enforcement officials and more-successful white bootleggers became part of African American cultural history and folklore.

During Prohibition, patterns of community policing and law enforcement formed that created de-facto legal protection for those African American communities willing to become the sensual and sexual playgrounds for the larger white community. In the South, law enforcement allowed illegal bootlegging in African American communities. In the North, the police allowed illegal speakeasies, prostitution, and drug use in the larger cities. Police occasionally raided African American businesses, but new ones opened up all the time. The African American community of Harlem flourished in New York City during Prohibition. Jervis Anderson (1981:42–45) provides the following comments: "Along Lennox Avenue liquor was to be obtained in the most unlikely of places, delicatessens, shoe shops, news stands. . . . There were really cheap speakeasies, stocking large amounts of moonshine behind a thin camouflage of legitimate business."

Harlem became famous for its jazz clubs, after-hours joints, gambling houses, and houses of prostitution. White New York discovered its dancing, music, poetry, art, and literature, and the Harlem Renaissance was born. While the nation endured a depression, in Harlem creativity kept pace with hunger, unemployment, and segregation. Many noted African American artists and writers such as Langston Hughes, Jacob Lawrence, and Ralph Ellison found their artistic beginnings there.

The new music called "jazz" was at the center of much of the excitement in urban African American life. Even though many of the clubs were still white-owned, there was a sense of pride and accomplishment among African Americans. African American soldiers had fought well in World War I and returned home to celebrate. Alcohol and drug use began to steadily increase. Jazz music, club life, and alcohol and drug use were not confined to the large East Coast cities. Eddie Rucker of Los Angeles, and later Seattle, was a comedian and musician who worked the West Coast clubs during this era. In the book *Jackson Street After Hours,* by Paul de Barros (1993:30), Rucker's peers describe him as a hard drinker and drug user: "Great? He sure was! The only thing Eddie had to get full of (was) his cocaine. He used to booze it down with whiskey. He liked them straight shots of Scotch, I sure remember that."

By 1928, alcohol consumption by African Americans had soared. A Metropolitan Life Insurance Company report stated that "The death rate per 100,000 from alcoholism steadily increased among Negro policyholders. And since 1911, in only one year, that of 1917 (a war year), was the rate higher than for the year 1927. In the past two years the rate increased from 4.12 to 5.3, while the rate for White policyholders declined from 3.1 to 2.8 per 100,000" (Carter 1928: 360).

African Americans had become caught up in the "party life" that was associated with the culture from which black urban music and dance evolved. Music and dance were becoming very popular across the nation and created highly visible African American celebrities. The African American community network shielded the illegal alcohol traffic, as well as the traffic in the newly popular drugs opium, marijuana, cocaine, and heroin. African American people, with legitimate reasons for distrusting the legal system that protected the interests of whites and the entrenched racial caste system, were often willing to protect the "dope man" with vows of silence. The antidrug laws, enacted after Prohibition as a part of the Harrison Act, attempted to control drinking in the African American community. These laws simply reinforced the opposition in the African American community because the use of alcohol had become part of the cultural, psychosocial, and economic life of African Americans in northern urban cities. In view of the fact that alcohol had become a part of the African American experience, it is not surprising that alcohol-related health problems began to emerge.

AFRICAN AMERICAN LIVER CIRRHOSIS MORTALITY

Cirrhosis mortality rates among African Americans were similar to the rates of the white population until the mid-fifties (Herd 1985), when this pattern changed, and African Americans experienced an epidemic of cirrhosis that exceeded the moderate increase among the white population. African American mortality rates increased as much as four times in urban coastal and northern areas and remained low in the southern rural areas. This pattern was reversed among whites, whose mortality rates were higher in the South. African American mortality rates appear to have been related to the increased association of the temperance movement with racial segregation and political disfranchisement of African Americans, in addition to the Great Migration of African Americans in the 1920s and 1930s to urban areas where alcohol was readily available.

At first, during the 1930s and 1940s, African American cirrhosis mortality rates were actually slightly below the rates of whites, but African American rates began to rise in the late 1940s. They surpassed the white rates, for both males and females, in 1955. Increases in mortality rates for African Americans and the general population during the 1950s, 1960s, and early 1970s occurred in conjunction with the rise in per capita consumption of alcohol.

From 1969 to 1971 the patterns changed for African Americans as the rates in the southern coastal areas rose to match the rates in the North, where there were more "wet" areas (ibid.). The centers in the coastal region with the highest mortality rates were the District of Columbia, Maryland, and Delaware—urbanized areas that saw major immigration of southern African Americans. African American mortality rates in the interior rural areas of the South remained low and comparable to white mortality rates. During the period from 1969 to 1971, African Americans in the North and in the South Atlantic regions were between three and four times more likely to die of cirrhosis than African Americans in the rural South (ibid.).

A 1981 report to the United States Congress on alcohol and health indicated that cirrhosis mortality rates for African Americans are disproportionately high, particularly in the seven major urban cities that account for half of the cirrhosis deaths among African Americans: Baltimore, Chicago, Detroit, Los Angeles, New York, Philadelphia, and Washington, D.C. In these cities, the rates among African American males between the ages of twenty-five and thirty-four are as much as ten times higher than for white males of the same age. For the general population, the cirrhosis mortality rate for African Americans is nearly twice that for white Americans (DeLuca 1981).

African American males are at extremely high risk for acute and chronic alcohol-related diseases such as cirrhosis, alcoholic fatty liver, hepatitis, heart disease, and cancers of the mouth, larynx, tongue, esophagus, and lung, in addition to accidental injuries and homicide (Herd 1989). One possible explanation for the high level of health problems among African American males may be the development of heavy drinking patterns later in life and the effects of poverty and poor education (Herd 1988b). In addition, there are possible differences in the biochemical vulnerability of African Americans to alcohol-related health problems in comparison to other populations. Studies of the relationship of biochemical markers and alcoholism in African Americans are few, and more research in this important area is needed (Behrens et al. 1988).

STUDIES OF PATTERNS OF ALCOHOL USE AMONG AFRICAN AMERICANS

Even though African Americans have been included in some national surveys of drinking patterns and problems, studies devoted to patterns of alcohol use among African Americans are a recent phenomenon. Of the sixteen thousand studies on alcohol use published from 1943 to 1973, only seventy-seven made reference to African Americans, and only eleven were specifically about African Americans (Brown and Tooley 1989). Very few studies have focused on African American cultural norms, values, beliefs, and behaviors (NIAAA 1980).

The first national survey of alcohol use that involved representative samples of African Americans and Latinos was conducted in 1984 (Clark and Hilton 1991). This survey found that African American and white men had similar drinking patterns, although more African American men abstained than white men (29 percent versus 23 percent) and white males tended to be heavier drinkers. The survey indicated that for women the same pattern existed, but with a larger margin of difference. African American women had higher abstinence rates than white women (46 percent versus 34 percent); white women were more likely to be heavier drinkers. However, when abstainers were excluded from the analysis, African American females comprised a slightly higher proportion of heavy drinkers. Important racial differences were found in relation to age groups. White males in the age group from eighteen to twenty-nine years drank more heavily, with heavy drinking declining in successive age groups. African American males aged eighteen to twenty-nine abstained more, with higher rates of heavy drinking among African American males in their thirties. White females in the eighteen to twenty-nine years age group were significantly more likely to drink, and to drink more heavily, than young African American females. (Further evidence corroborates the higher abstention rates among African American youth and young adults [Barnes and Welte 1986a, 1986b; Welte and Barnes 1987; Brown and Tooley 1989]).

The national survey found that, although overall drinking levels were lower among African Americans, African American males reported higher rates of alcohol-related problems (medical, personal, and social), with the exception of driving while intoxicated, which was more frequent among whites than African Americans. African American females reported fewer alcohol-related problems than white females, except for the slightly higher proportion of African American females with health problems. In the eighteen to twenty-nine years age group, white men were at highest risk for alcohol-related problems, while African American men were at lowest risk.

For men in their thirties, alcohol-related problem rates decreased sharply among whites but increased among African Americans. The results of a national study indicated that African American men between the ages of thirty and thirty-nine exceeded white men in the category of "frequent high maximum drinkers" by 33 to 26 percent (Herd 1989). African American men also more often became frequent heavy drinkers during their thirties and forties and also exceeded white men in frequent heavy drinking in the fifties and sixties age groups. In middle and older age, African Americans continued to experience alcohol use problems.

Analysis of the effect of socioeconomic variables on alcohol-related problem rates has found these factors to be more strongly correlated for African American males than white males. Among African American men, poor education, poverty, and heavy alcohol consumption were related to drinking problems. For white men, only consumption was related to drinking problems. The higher vulnerability to alcohol among African Americans may be due to socioeconomic factors, such as unemployment, adverse living conditions, poor health care, and racial discrimination (Herd 1988b). Research and public attention focused on alcoholism are on the rise, and this should result in heightened awareness of the complex factors involved. However, there is a need for much more research related specifically to alcoholism and African Americans, particularly women and adolescents, and it should include research on drinking patterns.

PREVENTION AND INTERVENTION ISSUES

Alcoholism is believed to be a disease, and as with any disease, certain social factors influence its etiology. Lifestyle, psychological frame of mind, social status, and available economic resources can be powerful determinants of who is affected by certain diseases. These factors can also influence the availability and quality of treatment programs and the prospects for recovery. The development of alcoholism is different for different racial and cultural groups, and the progression of the disease of alcoholism can be influenced by social and cultural factors.

Peter Bell and J. Evans's (1981) description of the disease stresses the importance of cultural factors in chemical dependency among African Americans. The authors argue that addiction is primary—that it is "the fundamental presenting problem for the individual." Though racism and oppression certainly contribute to alcohol abuse, Bell and Evans further argue that abuse is not a "secondary issue to . . . psychological and emotional problems . . . or just one factor resulting from racism and oppression." Unless the victim of the disease of addiction chooses to actively work on recovery, the addiction leads progressively, compulsively, and obsessively toward death (Schaef 1987).

To some degree, alcohol abuse in the African American community is a result of the effects of racism in America. Individual and institutional racism is a part of the American experience as it was a part of the constitutional paradigm on which the nation was founded. Some researchers believe it can be counterproductive for African Americans to overemphasize the importance of cultural factors and racism in the treatment of alcohol addiction; others believe race is a primary factor in the treatment of African Americans.

We believe it is essential for individuals involved in the prevention, intervention, or treatment of African American addicts to understand the important role of culture. It is also important to separate etiology from outcomes of the disease. While there do not appear to be common psychological characteristics that drive individuals to alcoholism, there does appear to be a set of psychological outcomes that characterize many alcoholics as the illness progresses. Frances L. Brisbane and Maxine Womble (1985) concluded that that there is no single set of psychological characteristics that account for all addictions but that significant personality factors appear to be present in all individuals who are addicted. These factors may be outcomes of addiction and include (1) seeking sensation and difficulty in postponing gratification; (2) a tendency toward nonconformity and lack of commitment; (3) antisocial behavior and social alienation; and (4) a lack of self-esteem, an elevated level of stress, and marked depression.

The complications that arise in treating African American alcoholics make treatment for African Americans more difficult and less effective, at least as treatment is conducted presently. These complications become readily apparent when the psychological consequences listed above are considered in light of social, political, and cultural factors operative within the African American community. These factors are as follows:

The history of racism in the United States and the psychological handicap it imposes on an individual's self-esteem;

Poverty, unemployment, and a lack of job and career opportunities;

The easy availability of drugs in African American communities;

The lure of selling drugs as a lucrative alternative career;

The hopelessness of ghetto life;

Lifestyles that reject menial or subsistence jobs in favor of hustling and the drama of dope dealing;

Cultural and class conflict;

Inadequate education and the dropout syndrome;

Frustration from continuing discrimination and rejection; and

The consistent or occasional use of alcohol by drug-addicted individuals as though alcohol is not a drug.

Such factors must be considered when planning prevention, intervention, and treatment programs for African Americans, especially those who reside in lower-income communities. If drug-using and -dealing behaviors by African Americans are viewed in the context of the lifestyle that lower-income people develop to cope with the factors listed above, then it becomes easier to understand these behaviors and provide effective programs.

As James Royce (1981) has pointed out,

[A]ny attempt to deal with alcohol problems in people of a particular culture must exhibit genuine sensitivity to the language, customs, and thinking of that culture. . . . success is contingent upon being recognized as one who understands and accepts them as they are. This involves study, comparison without condescension, and, above all, the ability to listen. (180)

Many white middle-class professionals who attempt to provide services to the African American client often have difficulty accepting and comprehending these factors. In this regard, there are four problematic attitudes that can serve as barriers to working with African Americans.

1. Bigotry. The professional is intolerant and rigidly devoted to his or her own group, religion, race, or politics. The professional believes consciously or unconsciously that the African American client is inferior and that his or her problems are a result of the outgrowth of feelings of racial inferiority. Pathological states are stressed, and strengths and adaptive behaviors are excluded from consideration.

2. Color Blindness. This is a belief by the white therapist that skin color is not important when working with the African American client, leading to a failure to realize that racism exists and rendering the professional helpless to deal with the client's personal experience related to prejudice against his or her skin color.

3. Paternalism. This attitude is characteristic of the poorly informed therapist who attributes all the problems of African Americans to society and the impact of racism. This professional views the African American individual as "culturally disadvantaged and deprived."

4. Compliance. The professional fears that a confrontation with the client might trigger the professional's underlying anger that is difficult to control and might expose hidden racism.

ALCOHOLISM TREATMENT

The Alcoholics Anonymous (AA) treatment approach, as a part of a comprehensive treatment plan of community-based services, has been effective in treating African Americans addicted to alcohol. The following story is quoted from the Big Book, the basic text for Alcoholics Anonymous, and is one of the stories that was added in 1955.

CASE STUDY
Another Chance

Poor, Black, totally ruled by alcohol, she felt shut away from any life worth living. But when she began a prison sentence, a door opened. I am an Afro-American alcoholic. I don't know when I became an alcoholic, but I do believe I became one because I drank too much too often. I always blamed my drinking on being poor, or on anything other than the truth—that I liked what booze did for me, that when I had a drink I was as big and had as much as the next person. I would never admit that I was drinking too much, or spending money that I should have used to buy food for my two little boys.

As time went on, I drank more. I was not able to hold a job— no one wants a drunk around. I was always able to get a boyfriend who had a drinking joint or sold whiskey, but it didn't last long. I would embarrass everyone by coming in drunk or passing out. Then it got to the place I couldn't drink without getting in jail. On one of these trips, the judge must have thought I was worth saving, for instead of sending me to jail, he sent me to A.A. for one month.

I went to A.A. At least, my body went. I hated every minute of it. I couldn't wait until the meeting was over to get a drink. I was afraid to drink before the meeting. I thought if they smelled whiskey on my breath, they would lock me up, and I couldn't live without my bottle. I hated that judge for sending me to a place with all those drunks. I wasn't an alcoholic!

Oh, I might drink too much at times—everyone I knew drank. But I don't remember that any of them ever went to sleep in joints and woke up with no shoes on in the winter, or fell out of chairs. But I did. I don't remember any of them getting put out in the winter because they didn't pay their rent. But to me, whiskey meant more than a home for my sons.

Things got so bad, I was afraid to go on the street, so I turned to Mother's Aid. That was one of the worst things that could have happened to an alcoholic woman. I would wait for the mailman each month, like any good mother, but as soon as he handed me my check, I put on my best dress and went looking for my alcoholic friend. Once I started drinking, I didn't care that the rent wasn't paid, or that there was no food in the house, or that my boys needed shoes. I would stay out until my money was gone. Then I would go home full of remorse, and wonder what I was going to do until I got my next check.

In time, I began to go out and forget the way back home. I would wake to find myself in some beat-up rooming house, where roaches were crawling over everything. Then the time came when I finally couldn't afford whiskey, so I turned to wine. Finally, I got so low-down, I was ashamed of my friends' seeing me, so I went to the worst joints I could find. If it was daylight, I would go down alleys to make sure no one saw me. My father was and still is a minister, and I was afraid that I might run into him, or that someone might tell him where I was, and I could still remember what he had done to me when I got drunk one Christmas when I was very young.

I felt that I didn't have anything to live for, so I tried suicide many times. But I would always wake up in the psychiatric ward to begin another long treatment. After a while, I found that the psycho ward was a good place to hide when I had taken something stolen to the pawnshop. I thought if the cops did come to the hospital, the doctors would tell them I was crazy and didn't know what I was doing. But then one good doctor told me there was nothing wrong with me except drinking too much. He said if I came back again, they would send me to the state hospital. I didn't want that, so I stopped going to the psycho ward.

Now I had gotten to the place where I would wake up with black eyes and not know where I got them, or wake up with lots of money and not know where I got it. Later, I found out that I went into stores and stole clothes, then sold them. One morning, I woke up with a thousand dollars. I was trying to remember where it came from, when two of the biggest cops I ever saw walked in and took me to jail. It came out that I had sold a woman a fur coat. The cops had picked her up, and she told them she had bought it from me. I got out on bail right away, but when I went to trial, the judge gave me thirty days. When my thirty days were up, I started back on my rounds. I didn't last long. They tell me that I killed a man during that period, but I can't remember anything. It was a total blackout.

Because I had been drunk, the judge gave me only a twelve-year sentence in prison.

By the grace of God, I only served three years. It was there that I really found out what A.A. was. I had rejected A.A. on the outside, but now it came to me in prison. Today, I thank my Higher Power for giving me another chance at life and A.A. and being able to try and help some other alcoholic. I have been home for a year, and have not taken a drink in four years.

Since I have been in A.A., I have more friends than I ever had in my life—friends who care about me and my welfare, friends who don't care that I am Black and that I have been in prison. All they care about is that I am a human being and that I want to stay sober. Since I've been home, I have been able to gain the respect of my two sons again. So many wonderful things have happened to me that at times I can't believe this is me. I think I am dreaming and will soon wake up.

The only thing that bothers me is that there are only about five

Negroes in A.A. in my city. Even those don't take part in A.A. functions as I would like to see them do. I don't know if it's force of habit or something else that keeps them in one place, but I do know that in A.A. there is much work to do, and none of us can do it standing still. I hope I haven't hurt anyone's feelings, but maybe we could all grow and change.

I do think that some of the Negroes here—and other places, too—are afraid to go to meetings. I just want to say that you don't have to be afraid, because no one at any A.A. meeting will bite you. There are no color bars in A.A. If you give us a try, you will see that we are really human beings, and we will welcome you with open arms and hearts. I am talking about A.A. people, who have gone through some of the same things that you might be going through now.

I'm writing this during an A.A. convention, where I have spent the weekend with nothing but white people. They haven't eaten me yet! I have not seen a Black face but mine since I've been here, and if I didn't look in the mirror, I wouldn't know that I was Black, because these people treat me as one of them, which I am. We all have the same sickness, and in helping one another, we are able to stay sober.

I am hoping that writing this may bring some poor, mixed-up soul into the program. It's time to stop finding excuses for drinking and getting into trouble, because now there is a way out, and if you want what we have, try coming around and giving the program a chance. (Alcoholics Anonymous 1976)

Although this story was written in the 1950s, there are similar recent stories of African Americans involved in AA as a part of their recovery program. It is particularly difficult for African Americans, who have felt alienated by a racist society, to identify with the culture of AA when the meetings are mostly white. African Americans living in urban areas have an easier time finding predominantly African American AA groups. It is also hard for African Americans when they begin to substitute recovery friends from non-African American backgrounds for their previous, alcohol-using African American friends who still want to be drinking buddies. African American women are showing up in increasing numbers in AA, but are also attending predominantly African American churches in larger numbers and are often trying to recover through communion with God, the minister, or friends instead of AA. Many middle-class African Americans try to keep their struggle with alcoholism a secret, even from family members. Middle-class African Americans are often unwilling to attend AA meetings because they fear that their status will be affected by public disclosure. This fear of public disclosure is also faced by middle-class white alcoholics.

In the early 1970s, the National Institute on Alcohol Abuse and Alcoholism (NIAAA) was established in addition to a variety of alcohol-specific treatment agencies and programs across the country. These agencies (NIAAA-funded alcoholism treatment centers and special population programs) now form the core of institutions for dealing with alcohol-related problems. A survey of these agencies indicated that African Americans are disproportionately represented in alcohol treatment programs (NIAAA 1980, 1983).

One treatment method valued by practitioners working with African American alcoholics is outreach counseling, because many clients are not likely to come into agencies for alcoholism treatment. Deterrents include historical segregation, feelings of isolation, and the view that excessive alcohol consumption is not a serious problem that requires professional assistance. Some African Americans who drink heavily are more concerned about social problems, such as job loss and family conflict, that might result from drinking rather than health problems associated with the disease. African American families sometimes feel that they can handle the problem by treating the symptoms of heavy drinking at home with homemade remedies.

A good treatment model for African Americans includes staff training about African American cultural and drinking patterns and education and outreach services that involve the family, outpatient and inpatient care, emergency care, halfway house resources, and program evaluation. This treatment model incorporates families, communities, and churches.

ALCOHOLISM AND AFRICAN AMERICAN WOMEN

Frederick Harper (1976) reported that 51 percent of African American women abstain from alcohol, for the following reason: (1) responsibility for the family and for keeping their drinking husbands and men out of trouble, (2) parental and religious teaching that "nice ladies" don't drink, (3) dislike of the bitter and dry tastes of alcoholic beverages, and (4) the lack of access to liquor due to a tendency to stay at home rather than participate in drinking. As mentioned previously, in a review of drinking patterns and alcohol-related problems among African Americans conducted as part of a national survey, Dennis Herd (1991) found that 46 percent of the African American women in the sample were abstainers, compared to 34 percent of white women. Generally, African American women reported fewer alcohol-related problems of any kind, compared to white women. The differences were especially strong in the areas of driving while drunk (2.1 percent versus 10.8 percent), belligerence (4.7 percent versus 8.6 percent), and financial problems (1.0 percent versus 2.7 percent). This same study indicated that increases in income for African American women were generally associated with a decline in abstention and an increase in frequent drinking. African American women with yearly incomes ranging from $6,000 to $10,000 dollars abstained at the rate of 44 percent, whereas African American women with incomes ranging from $20,000 to $30,000 abstained at a rate of 29 percent. African American women in the eighteen to twenty-nine years age group were less likely than white women to drink at all, to drink frequently, or to drink at high maximum levels (Herd 1991).

Jerome Taylor and Beryl Jackson (1990) evaluated the extent to which eight variables—life events, social support, religious orientation, internalized radicalism, physical health problems, marital status, socioeconomic status, and developmental status—accounted for differences in alcohol consumption. They found that life events, physical health problems, and internalized racism were important factors relating to alcohol consumption. While these studies have added to the knowledge base on drinking patterns and behaviors, further research on the contributing factors leading to alcohol-related problems among African American women is needed. Additional studies should address the age factor, as younger African American women appear to be at lower risk for problems associated with alcohol use. However, it is not known how age is related to cultural experiences, social factors, or geographic location. Because African American women at higher income levels have a lower rate of abstention than women at the lower income levels, an increase in knowledge about how income, as well as age, influences drinking patterns in African American women will affect prevention and intervention measures.

ALCOHOLISM AND AFRICAN AMERICAN YOUTH

Frederick Harper (1988) suggests nine propositions concerning African American youth and alcohol consumption. These propositions are as follows:

1. African American youth who drink may be imitating the drinking patterns they have observed in adults.

2. African American youth have lower rates of drinking due to their religious background, less money for alcohol, or less access to transportation to drinking places.

3. The prevalence of liquor stores in African American residential neighborhoods and near schools creates greater accessibility to alcohol and increases the risk of use.

4. African American youth often grow up with conflicting messages to drink heavily or not at all.

5. African American youth often find their nights on the streets turning into a way of life that leads to alcohol use.

6. African American youth have a lack of knowledge about alcohol and its consequences as well as a lack of community consensus about how, when, and where to use alcohol.

7. Patterns of use among African American youth are more a function of geography (urban vs. rural), age, religious orientation, gender, and family attitudes about alcohol than a function of race, which may become more of an influencing factor as youth become adults.

8. Choosing to drink and what to drink are very much influenced by racially oriented advertisements in African American magazines, on television, and on billboards in the African American residential communities.

9. Working parents and single parents frequently create an empty-home situation, which allows African American youth to get involved in partying and using alcohol during school hours, especially on Fridays or other special occasions (a behavior observed more often in urban areas).

It is not clear why African American youth have lower rates of involve-ment with alcohol compared to white youth. One significant factor for some African American youth is closer family involvement and more parental control. In addition, a greater awareness of the problems of alcohol (perhaps because of a family member with a drinking problem) and the influence of the church are other important factors that affect the rate of involvement with alcohol among African American youth. As African Americans reach their thirties and separate more from family and parental influences and the church, there is a tendency to consume more alcohol, especially as income, opportunity, and status increase.

A study of patterns of alcohol consumption among suburban Afri-can American high school youth found that African American youth drink smaller quantities less frequently than white youth, are more likely to be nondrinkers, are less likely than whites to drive while drunk, are twice as likely as whites to report never having been drunk, and are less likely to use alcohol for relief of physical pain, stress, or sleeplessness (Beck and Zannis 1992). Inner-city African American youth have also been found to drink less than other minorities (Welte and Barnes 1987). On the other hand, African American adults over thirty years of age are more likely than white adults to have higher rates of alcohol involve-ment, alcohol-related behaviors, and alcohol-related diseases such as cirrhosis of the liver and esophageal cancers (Report of the Secretary's Task Force on Black and Minority Health 1986).

This difference in drinking between youth and adults can be ex-plained in part by developmental issues. L. M. King (1981) reported that dependency and depression were the most common disorders in the African American population in the studies he reviewed. The most meaningful dimensions of depression in African American men were cognitive-affective impairment, retarded depression, and escapism (Steer and Shaw 1977), and Erik H. Erikson (1982) maintains that the failed attempt at intimacy results in isolation, the core of adult pathology. These symptoms are not uncommon for African American men who have not achieved life success in career expectations or marriage and who at age thirty begin to evaluate their future by looking at perceived past failures in work and love. These thoughts and feelings of failure result in some form of crisis and personal disorganization and may result in the use of alcohol as an escape mechanism. The onset of heavy drink-ing by African American men around age thirty is further exacerbated by the midlife crisis of the forties and the unresolved issues related to family and work.

While limited data on the patterns and problems of alcohol have been gathered on African American males, and to some extent African American females, the use of alcohol among African American male juvenile delinquents has been the subject of a few studies. Mary S. Jackson (1992) studied alcohol and other drug use patterns among African American juvenile delinquents in a large metropolitan area and found that 90 percent of the youth had used drugs, between 30 and 46 percent reported daily use, and the average age of initial use was about twelve years old. Alcohol use tended to precede by about five months the use of other illicit drugs. Over 70 percent of the youth reported that their fathers did not live at home, while about 20 percent stated that their mother was absent from home. Robbery accounted for just over 25 percent of the arrests, aggravated burglary, assault, and car theft for 17.7 percent, 16.1 percent, and 13.7 percent, respectively, of the remaining offenses. The mean age of initial alcohol use was twelve and a half years, and almost 90 percent of the youth reported using alcohol by the age of fifteen years.

The majority of these youth indicated that they used drugs to feel good (65 percent), while other significant reasons included taking drugs to feel like an adult and because of the influence of friends. Since, on the average, African American male juvenile delinquents begin using alcohol and other drugs at about twelve years of age, drug prevention and intervention programs must be available to African American males at the elementary school level before they begin to experiment with alcohol and other drugs. Additional research with African American female juvenile delinquents is needed in order to explore their patterns of alcohol use and to provide information for prevention programs.

ADVERTISING OF ALCOHOL

One factor related to African American alcoholism is the advertising of alcoholic beverages in the African American community on television, radio, billboards, and scoreboards, in newspapers and magazines, during car races, and on toys and games, matchbook covers, and tee shirts. These advertisements are everywhere in the African American community and the advertisers have little concern about ethics, decency, and fairness in the promotion of alcoholic beverages. Marketing techniques range from beer and wine posters on storefront windows in the immediate vicinity of elementary and secondary schools to billboards advertising alcohol products in areas well traveled by students. The alcohol industry has targeted the younger population of African Americans because it is experiencing a faster rate of growth than the white youth population. Concerns about these advertising practices are complicated by the fact that the alcoholic beverage industry often provides support for important African American community events and activities such as parades, celebrations, and scholarship programs for youth.

Although African American communities are saturated with alcohol advertising aimed at youth, the rate of alcohol-related problems and alcohol consumption remains low among African American youth because of the protective factors of family, community, and church. However, as African Americans become older the protective factors appear to become less influential.

In 1981, a network of eighty-seven African American newspapers in seventy-eight markets with more than four million urban consumers courted the alcohol industry to advertise in their membership publications (Alcohol Information Research Services 1987). Before this initiative the alcohol industry had used four major African American magazines—*Ebony, Black Enterprise, Jet*, and *Essence*—as outlets for advertisements of alcoholic beverages (Strickland et al. 1982). A content analysis of alcoholic beverage advertising in a total of forty-two magazines published in 1978, including the four magazines mentioned above, found that about 12 percent of the ads in the sample of African American–oriented magazines were for alcohol, nearly twice that expected "under the assumption of uniform distribution of ads across magazine types" (ibid.). Another study found that African American magazines had a higher-than-average concentration of alcohol advertisements, with one appearing on the average of every fifteen pages (ibid.).

Recent cases support the claim that the alcoholic beverage industry targets and promotes the themes of alcohol, sex, hedonism, and violence. St. Ides malt liquor commercials state:

Get your girl in the mood quicker, and get your jimmy thicker with
St. Ides liquor.

and

Tell your man to get you a six pack and don't be afraid of what it
does to you . . . 'cause it will get you in the mood . . .

The first quote was initially broadcast in June 1991 on a nationally syn-
dicated television show, "Pump It Up!" This late-night program on rap
and contemporary music, starring rappers and rock stars and a very
young host, targets African American youth. The second quote is from
a St. Ides radio commercial featuring Yo Yo, a young African American
female rapper (*Essence*, December 1991).

These St. Ides commercials and other alcoholic beverage advertisements that target the African American community often link alcohol
with sex but do not warn young African Americans that increased risks
of sexually transmitted diseases, sexual assault, and date rape are associated with drinking alcoholic beverages. In fact, the Bureau of Alcohol,
Tobacco and Firearms prohibits linking alcohol products with sex, and
these advertisements are in direct violation of such regulations.

The alcoholic beverage industry provides extensive support across
the nation for the celebration of the birthday of Dr. Martin Luther King,
Jr. Miller Brewing Company has sponsored and provided advertisements
in celebration of Black History Month (Hacker et al. 1987) and in 1987
established the Thurgood Marshall Scholarship for African American
youth, worth between $1.6 million and $2.0 million (*Ebony*, September
1991: 32). Since 1979, Anheuser-Busch has sponsored the Lou Rawls
Parade of Stars telethon to raise funds for the United Negro College Fund
and also sponsors an annual luncheon for the National Conference of
Black Mayors. Coors had a very negative experience in 1984 when the
chairman and chief executive officer made racist remarks about African
Americans to a meeting of minority businessmen in Denver, Colorado.
After an uproar and denouncements of Coors and a call for a nationwide boycott of Coors products by the African American community,
Coors made a commitment to spend over $625 million over five years
in African American and Latino communities to improve its image
among these groups (Hacker et al. 1987: 34). African Americans have
been hired in positions of visibility as vice presidents in charge of minority markets, public relations, and plant operations by Anheuser-

Busch, Miller Brewing, and Coors. African American advertising agencies have been hired by many alcoholic beverage companies to promote their products in African American communities.

The Liquor Handbook (1982) indicates that

> a highly significant, well-educated black middle-class is emerging that has a definite influence on the wine and spirits market. The most popular categories in the market in general are scotch, gin, vodka, rum, bourbon, sweet wines, and malt liquor. Stated in another way, 1 in 5 bottles of scotch are sold to black consumers, 2 in 5 bottles of gin, and 1 in 8 bottles of cognac. Blacks know what they're buying, buy top brands in the categories and have no problem with the fact that top brands cost more (142).

In this segment of the market are the members of the groups and businesses, such as the NAACP, the National Urban League, the seven major African American PanHellenic or Greek letter organizations, predominantly black churches, and civic organizations, that receive financial support from the alcoholic beverage industry. Thus, the African American middle-class and the organizations it supports hesitate to speak out against the serious health problems among African Americans caused by excessive consumption of alcoholic beverages.

CONCLUSION

We have examined a range of issues and problems associated with African American alcohol use in the United States, including traditions and norms, the impact of slavery, the Great Migration to the North, patterns of alcohol use, morbidity and mortality rates, prevention and intervention issues, racism, alcoholism treatment, alcoholism and African American women, alcoholism and African American youth, alcoholism and male African American juvenile delinquents, and advertising of alcohol that targets the African American community. We know that African American and European American men have different drinking patterns, and that African American women have higher abstinence rates than European American women. African American males experience acute and chronic medical, personal, and social problems associated with the heavy drinking of alcohol and are at very high risk for alcohol-related diseases such as cirrhosis of the liver, esophageal cancer, alcoholic fatty liver, and hepatitis.

Outreach counseling is valuable for practitioners working with African American clients because isolation and problem denial prevent many of these clients from seeking help at a community agency. A good treatment model would include information for staff about African American culture and drinking patterns and education and outreach services that include the family, outpatient and inpatient care, emergency care, halfway-house resources, church and community resources, employment opportunities, and the availability of Alcoholics Anonymous and other support groups.

Developing effective intervention strategies for alcohol-related problems in African Americans will require cultural competencies that include knowledge of the etiology of such problems in the African American population. Most practitioners lack this kind of knowledge because there are few studies with significant numbers of African Americans in the samples or subsamples. Seldom do these analyses provide information about the historical patterns of alcohol use and the psycho-social processes that have influenced alcohol-related problems in African Americans. Examining these issues will have important implications for developing appropriate strategies for prevention, intervention, and treatment of alcoholism in the African American community.

4 CIGARETTES AND MARIJUANA

African American adolescents appear to progress through several stages of drug involvement: beer and wine, cigarettes, hard liquor, marijuana, and finally, other illicit drugs.

—Brook, Hamburg, Balka, and Wynn 1992

The theory that among youth in general drug use evolves in stages, beginning with cigarettes (or other tobacco products), alcohol, and marijuana, and progressing to other drugs is known as the gateway theory of drug use (Kandel 1975). Cigarettes and marijuana get significant exposure and use in the African American community, and this chapter details the impact of these gateway drugs on African Americans. Tobacco companies target minorities because whites have been kicking the habit at a much faster rate. Almost 44 percent of African American adults smoke cigarettes, compared to 37 percent of whites, according to Simmons Market Research Bureau (D. Johnson 1992: 26–28).

CIGARETTES

Cigarettes, which contain nicotine, are a very powerful, addictive drug. The number of smokers in the general population has declined. According to Dennis Breo (1993: 5), between 1965—when the Surgeon General's office issued its first warning—and 1991, smoking among all adults declined from 42.4 percent to 25.5 percent. Nevertheless, smoking continues to be a widespread addiction that affects forty-six million Americans.

Nicotine addiction is lethal, as the average male smoker in the United States loses eight years of life expectancy. Because the tobacco industry is losing older customers, it is focusing marketing efforts on finding more consumers among youth. It is estimated that, if the industry replaces yearly those who quit smoking and those who die from smoking-related diseases, there is a need for more than two million new smokers per year just to maintain current sales levels.

The number of teens smoking has not declined since 1980, and it is during this age period that the addiction usually begins. Approximately 90 percent of all smokers start before age eighteen, the average age for new smokers is thirteen, and each day five thousand teenagers start smoking for the first time (ibid.).

The federal Centers for Disease Control and Prevention concluded that nationally in 1990 there were 418,690 premature deaths (before age sixty-five) attributable to cigarette smoking in the United States alone (ibid.). While overall adult tobacco addiction rates are dropping in the United States, the smoking rates among African Americans are higher than among whites (D. Johnson 1992), and their death rates from tobacco are twice as high. However, African Americans tend to smoke fewer cigarettes daily and to begin smoking at a later age.

Smoking is a potent economic force—the Tobacco Institute estimated 1992 tobacco sales at $47.5 billion (Breo 1993). The tobacco industry casts a wide net of economic and political influence in the African American community that has a devastating effect. In Harlem, alcohol- and tobacco-related illnesses are the leading cause of death, deaths from heart disease in central Harlem are running 40 percent above the national average, and cancer rates are 65 percent above the national average. Yet the benefits of tobacco are advertised widely in the African American community—in store windows, in subway and bus stations, and on billboards in the streets—and African American members of Congress representing the area receive tens of thousands of dollars from the tobacco lobbies. Tobacco companies, like alcohol producers, have historically been major contributors to African American organizations in need of revenue and support, such as the National Urban League, the United Negro College Fund, and Operation PUSH. They also provide money for scholarship programs and to cover the costs of special events such as music festivals, conferences, fraternity and so-rority activities, performances of dance companies, fashion fairs, and commemorations of historical events (Coughlin 1992: 11).

In 1989, R. J. Reynolds Tobacco Company spent $10 million developing a high-tar menthol cigarette called Uptown to test-market in Philadelphia's African American community (Johnson 1992). However, the company underestimated the surprisingly swift and powerful reaction of the community and was forced to cancel its plans. Tobacco companies continue to target African American communities with special advertising and marketing strategies because African Americans are kicking the smoking habit at a slower rate than the general population. Unfortunately, a major effort to reduce or eliminate allegiances to alcohol and tobacco companies and dependence on cigarettes has yet to become a priority for African Americans. Until this happens, the health of the African American community continues to be controlled and determined by alcohol and tobacco companies and the addictive power of their products.

MARIJUANA

Marijuana is the Spanish name for *Cannabis sativa,* a green, strong-smelling plant that grows wild all over the world and is more commonly known as hemp. It has been used for thousands of years to make rope, cloth, and paper. The oil of hemp seeds is used in varnish and paint, and the seeds are used as bird food. The leaves and flowers of marijuana contain a chemical called THC, and medical scientists are finding ways to use THC to help people with eye problems, cancer, and HIV/AIDS.

However, THC can damage the mind and body when not used properly. All forms of cannabis have negative physical and mental effects (U.S. Department of Education 1992). The type of marijuana grown in Mexico is stronger than the kind that grows wild in the United States because the warmer weather causes the Mexican plant to produce more THC. Because of the recognized danger of the drug, in 1937 the U.S. Congress passed the Marijuana Tax Act, which labeled the drug a narcotic and made it illegal. Owning marijuana became a serious crime, but this did not stop use of the drug. David Solomon (1966: xiv) reports that prior to the Marijuana Tax Act "poor, segregated minority groups, especially Mexican-Americans and urban Negroes, used marijuana's consciousness-expanding properties as an economical euphoriant: its preparation does not entail fermentation or distillation; hence it is far cheaper to produce than alcoholic beverages."

During the period from October 1939 through November 1940, the New York Police Department arrested 167 people for the possession and use of marijuana, including 83 African American men and 6 African American women (Solomon 1966). At this time, there was also speculation that there were a few marijuana smokers among junior high and high school students of African American background, but it was concluded by most authorities that marijuana smoking was not a widespread practice among school children and youth in New York City.

In the 1960s, as the United States went through a time of rapid social change, the laws regarding marijuana use were thought by many to be unjust and unfair and were repealed in many states. African American and other soldiers in the Vietnam War began smoking marijuana because it was easy to get and was very strong. In 1970, Congress passed the Comprehensive Drug Abuse Prevention and Control Act, and marijuana was no longer considered a narcotic but a hallucinogen or mind-altering drug. This reclassification made the laws against its use less strict but did not make it legal to use the drug. The use of marijuana that began in the 1960s continues to increase for African American adults and teenagers.

Interviews with and observations of African Americans who have used marijuana indicate that the typical physical effects of marijuana use include a substantial increase in heart rate, bloodshot eyes, dry mouth and throat, and increased appetite. Users also report impairment of short-term memory and comprehension, an altered state of time and space, and a reduced ability to concentrate and coordinate tasks such as driving a car or operating machinery. Other problems include the inability to retain information when "high," a loss of motivation, altered thought processes, and possible paranoia and psychosis. African American users of marijuana, which contains cancer-causing chemical agents, inhale the unfiltered smoke deeply into their lungs and hold it as long as possible, damaging their pulmonary systems. Long-time users tend to develop a psychological tolerance that requires more of the drug to achieve the same effect. Some long-term African American users who have entered recovery programs report that the drug became the center of their lives.

Marijuana is easily available and inexpensive. It is used in order to feel relaxed or "mellow" and is a popular drug with teenagers. Nonusing African American youths report that because the side effects of the drug do not show up right away, users think marijuana is harmless. Other African American youths say that they need marijuana to relax, as the following story about two African American high school females demonstrates.

> During lunch break, Shawnda told her friend April that she was real nervous about going to a party with Malik, "a real handsome dude." April reached into her backpack and said: "I have something right here that will help you relax and have a good time tonight." She took out a small plastic container with a joint of marijuana in it and said, "Let's go over to the parking lot behind those cars and have a hit."
>
> Shawnda thought about it and felt that a hit or two would help her relax and enjoy the party. But she said, "What if I get too stoned and act stupid in front of Malik?" April punched Shawnda lightly on the arm and said, "Don't be silly, I'm not going to let you smoke the whole thing, just a couple of hits." Shawnda thought about it. Before she could decide, April said, "Hey, my parents share a joint every night after being stressed with work all day and it mellows them right out!" Shawnda said, "Do your parents smoke in front of you?" April said, "Sure, how do you think I got this stuff?" Shawnda thought again and reached for the joint, figuring that if it was cool for April's mom and dad, then it was cool for her.

RESEARCH ON MARIJUANA USE

Research studies on the use of marijuana among African Americans are few. The research that does exist indicates that African American youth generally have lower rates of marijuana use than whites. In the 1990 National Household Survey, the prevalence for marijuana use was 13 percent for African American adolescents, compared to 16 percent for white adolescents (NIDA 1991). African American males in the National Seniors Survey (Bachman et al. 1991) had a level of current marijuana use of 9 percent compared to 25 percent for whites, and African American females in the survey had a similar rate. However, survey rates of marijuana use may be artificially low for African Americans if they are based on school attendance because such surveys do not include African Americans involved in disciplinary actions that result in school suspension, the rate of which is higher for African Americans than for other students. In addition, the rate of marijuana use varies among different populations of African Americans and reflects their different circumstances—poverty, homelessness, lack of hope, and lack of job opportunities are factors that often play a part in marijuana use. For example, Norweeta Milburn and Jacqueline Booth (1992) compared the lifetime, annual, and current prevalence of illicit drug and alcohol use among 358 homeless African American adults with the prevalence estimates for nonhomeless African Americans from the general population. They found that across all age categories homeless African American adults were more likely than other African Americans to have used marijuana in their lifetimes. Lifestyle, self-esteem, church attendance or a sense of spirituality, social supports, participation in meaningful activities, peer use of marijuana, and overall well-being all can influence whether or not an individual uses marijuana. African American males, especially, are more vulnerable to negative factors that put them at risk.

Kenneth Maton and Marc Zimmerman (1992) analyzed three sets of variables—lifestyle, social support/stress, and well-being—to predict frequency of alcohol, marijuana, and hard drug use among 150 African American males from inner-city Baltimore. The prevalence rates for illicit substance use among this sample were higher than the national average. Lifestyle was a significant predictor of marijuana and other drug use, and low self-esteem predicted increased marijuana use six months later. Among individual predictor values in cross-sectional analysis (with all predictor variables entered), independent variance in substance use was explained by school status (whether an individual was in school or a dropout) for alcohol and marijuana use, by spirituality for marijuana and hard drug use, and by life event stress for marijuana use. Lifestyle predictor variables were school status, spirituality, and self-perceived participation in meaningful activities as measured on a five-point Likert scale. The results suggested that a lifestyle that included an adaptive compensatory behavioral outlet such as church attendance may be more protective than a lifestyle that does not include compensatory behavior. Youths who dropped out of high school before graduation but were involved in meaningful activity reported less alcohol and substance use than youths who left school and were not so involved.

In 1987, the National Institute of Justice established the Drug Use Forecasting (DUF) program as a way of measuring the extent of drug use by persons charged with criminal behavior in major American cities. The DUF program uses urinalysis results (an objective measure) to determine the types and levels of drug use by this segment of the population in twenty-four major cities. The 1992 DUF statistics report on male arrestees (Department of Justice 1992) indicates that 77 percent of the arrestees in Chicago were African Americans in their twenties and thirties, and 69 percent had tested positive for drug use generally. The statistical report does not break down marijuana use by race, but among all male arrestees marijuana use was at 26 percent. When compared to other drugs, marijuana use was second only to cocaine use, which was at 56 percent. In Washington, D.C., a total of 93 percent of all male arrestees were African American, as were 89 percent of all female arrestees. Marijuana use for all male arrestees (regardless of race) was at 20 percent, and for all female arrestees marijuana use was at 8 percent. For all male arrestees marijuana use was exceeded only by cocaine use, and for all female arrestees marijuana use was exceeded by use of cocaine and the opiates. In Los Angeles, a total of 35 percent of all male arrestees were African American, and 43 percent of all female arrestees were African American. Marijuana use for all male arrestees was at 23 percent, and for all female arrestees at 13 percent. For all male and female arrestees, marijuana use was exceeded only by cocaine use. These sample findings from Chicago, Washington, D.C., and Los Angeles indicate that African Americans in general are overrepresented in the arrested populations in major cities. African American males are arrested at a two-to-one ratio to other males, and African American females at a three-to-one ratio to other females. It is worth noting also that male arrestees use marijuana at a rate twice that of female arrestees. Additional research based on Drug Use Forecasting statistics is needed to determine whether African American female arrestees are using marijuana at a lower rate than African American male arrestees.

The National Institute on Drug Abuse (NIDA) has given considerable attention to documenting the use of marijuana because marijuana has been and continues to be the most widely used illicit drug in this country. Among members of the household population age twelve or older, African American males were the most likely to have ever used marijuana (41.4 percent) and to have used it in the past month (8.7 per-cent). For instance, among those age twelve to seventeen, white males were most likely to have used marijuana in the past month, but among those aged twenty-six to thirty-four, African American males were more likely to have used marijuana in the past month (NIDA 1990).

Annual Emergency Room Data reports (NIDA 1991) are generated from the Drug Abuse Warning Network (DAWN), which is sponsored by NIDA. The weighted estimates are based on data submitted by a representative sample of 502 nonfederal short-stay general surgical and medical hospitals with twenty-four-hour facilities. In 1991, 27 percent of emergency room (ER) drug abuse patients were African Americans. This rate is approximately twice the percentage of African Americans in the general population. Individuals twenty-five years of age or younger accounted for 26 percent of African American patients. ER estimates for marijuana/hashish episodes were reported for 5.3 percent of African American patients, the highest rate for any racial/ethnic group.

DAWN data are limited in several respects. The data are collected only for those drug abuse occurrences that have resulted in a medical crisis and subsequently have been identified as drug abuse episodes by a facility reporting to DAWN, and reporting on these episodes may reflect drug use self-reported by the patient to attending medical staff. Thus, the data on African American use of marijuana/hashish at 5.3 percent is an estimate only for this segment of the African American population. Also, the number of ER episodes reported to DAWN is not equivalent to the number of individuals involved, since one individual may make several visits to an ER. DAWN data contain no personal identifiers, which would be required to eliminate repeat data entries of the same individual. As mentioned previously, other estimates by NIDA of marijuana use by African American youth range from 9 to 13 percent of African American adolescents.

Some African American youth sell cocaine to get money to buy marijuana and clothes and to support themselves and their families. These youth often smoke marijuana and drink "forty ouncers" of beer, may have an addiction to money and gambling, and may be "closet smokers" of crack cocaine. Others are involved in male prostitution and other illegal activities in order to get drugs. Another danger is the smoking of "sherms" (marijuana soaked in embalming fluid), which reportedly have the impact of a Sherman tank. One young African American described his experience with sherms as "having his legs on the first floor while his body was walking around on the third floor."

A study of 919 urban African American, European American, and Asian American fifth graders examined family risk factors that predict early alcohol, tobacco, and marijuana initiation (Catalano et al. 1992). Initiation was highest among European Americans, followed by African Americans, and lowest among Asian Americans. A statistical analysis revealed significant differences by ethnicity in family management practices, involvement in family activities, sibling deviancy, parental disapproval of children's drinking, and family structure.

To study the effects of marijuana use on adolescent personality, attitudinal and behavioral attributes, perceived parent-adolescent relations, and perceived peer factors in African American and white adolescents, questionnaires were administered to 693 high school students (292 African American, 401 white) in the ninth and tenth grades and again two years later (Brook et al. 1989). The results indicated that regular use of marijuana may lead to lower achievement, increased tolerance of deviance, more deviant behavior, and greater rebelliousness. The results also indicated that regular use of marijuana seems to interfere with the relationships between adolescents and their parents and leads to association with adolescents who are using drugs and engaging in more deviant behavior. The consequences of marijuana use were generally similar in the different gender and age groups, but there were some ethnic differences, as marijuana use had a greater impact on whites than African Americans. In this study, social class differences were eliminated by selecting a predominantly middle-class sample. However, it can be speculated that the African American middle-class students were probably less vulnerable to the effects of marijuana use because of stronger family and community support systems.

W. David Watts and Lloyd S. Wright (1990) examined the relationship between drug use and delinquent behavior among high school males confined to a maximum security facility for violent and repeat offenders. Self-administered questionnaires were analyzed separately for each racial subgroup. The analysis revealed that self-reported alcohol, tobacco, marijuana, and other illegal drug use were all significantly related to both minor and violent delinquency for all racial subgroups, including African Americans. In this study, the best predictors of violent delinquency for African American males were the frequent use of illegal drugs, including marijuana.

Interviews with African American youth who started using marijuana during their preteen years indicated that they were not aware of what was happening to them when they first used marijuana. They reported being disoriented, with a heightened sense of awareness and a loss of memory. For African Americans, as well as others, marijuana diminishes the left brain functions of logical thinking, reasoning, and rational processes and increases the right brain functions of emotions, creativity, and introspection. Marijuana also affects the ability of users to read and comprehend written material. Thus, school-age youth who smoke marijuana regularly have difficulty with their academic coursework.

In a study of adolescent substance use among 135 African American, Hispanic, Asian, and white students in middle schools and high schools in Los Angeles County, it was found that African Americans showed the highest level of smoking cigarettes and the lowest level of alcohol and other drug use (Maddahian, Newcomb, and Bentler 1986). The study was limited by a sample that represents only one geographical area and generalizations to other areas must be made with caution. However, this study and a follow-up study stressed considering social and environmental factors, including family, cultural, and ethnic values, the availability of drugs, and drug-using friends. Knowledge of these areas would assist in the development of prevention and treatment programs for African American adolescents (ibid.).

African Americans who smoke marijuana risk becoming dependent on the drug. The belief that addiction runs in African American families requires additional research, but there is evidence to suggest that genetic factors are very influential in the predisposition for marijuana addiction. An individual's genetic endowment contains a set of "instructions" that guide the individual's growth and development. These are often referred to as predispositions, and the outcome will depend on the environment and life circumstances in which the individual is placed or puts himself or herself. Thus, some people tend to have addictive types of personalities, and this tendency may be genetic. Interviews with African Americans who have become marijuana users indicate that marijuana is addictive for some and not for others. One hit of marijuana for one individual may be the gateway drug that leads to heroin, crack cocaine, and other drug addictions. This is the real and inherent danger in the use of marijuana or other drugs by African American youth who are in dysfunctional family or community circumstances. For many African Americans, marijuana represents a way of masking the pain of poverty, oppression, lack of hope, and lack of opportunities. Many African Americans try to fill the spiritual emptiness in their lives with the medicating effect of marijuana and other drugs.

TREATMENT

In recent times, a wide variety of treatments or cures for drug abuse have been proposed or attempted, including incarceration in mental institutions and detainment in prison. These approaches had limited success until 1935, when two alcoholics found that they could do something together that they could not do alone. This was the beginning of Alcoholics Anonymous (AA). In 1953, the same principles led to the formation of Narcotics Anonymous (NA). In the 1970s, Marijuana Anonymous was founded based on AA and NA principles, and it pioneered a new way of life for many marijuana addicts. However, African Americans are not participating in Marijuana Anonymous in significant numbers, perhaps because of the attitude that marijuana is a "softer" drug than crack cocaine or heroin.

Detoxification is the process by which the body discharges the toxins accumulated from years of marijuana use. The process begins to happen the first few days or weeks after becoming clean and sober. Detoxification is also the process of adjusting to dealing with real feelings and the reality of life without self-medicating or numbing. Despite the research that indicates there are no physiological effects from marijuana addiction, many recovering African American members of Marijuana Anonymous report definite withdrawal symptoms. Whether the causes of these withdrawal symptoms are physical or psychological, the results are physical symptoms. Other recovering members have had emotional and mental adjustment problems as they stop using marijuana. Essentially, there is no way to determine who will have physical discomfort and who will not. Most members report minor physical discomfort, but others report no physical withdrawal symptoms. The most common symptom of withdrawal from marijuana is insomnia, lasting from a few nights to a few months of very little sleep. Depression is the next most common symptom, followed by nightmares and vivid dreams. Marijuana tends to dampen the dreaming process, so dreams often come back vividly and intensely after stopping the use of marijuana, an effect that may last for years. The fourth most common symptom is anger, ranging from a slow-burning irritability to sudden bursts of unexpected rage. This includes anger at the world, family, friends, and self and anger about being addicted to marijuana and having to get clean. Emotional highs and lows are common, ranging from depression to anger to euphoria. On occasion, recovering addicts experience feelings of fear and anxiety, a loss of their sense of humor, and decreased or increased sex drive during the first few months of detoxification. Most of these symptoms fade to normal levels after about three months, but the loss of concentration and the inability to read, remember, and learn is very common during the early months of recovery.

The most common physical symptom of withdrawal from marijuana reported by African Americans is headaches for a few weeks or months. These headaches can be very intense over the first few days. The next most common physical symptom is night sweats, as the body discharges toxins. Night sweats can last from a few nights to a month and may be accompanied by hand sweats and body odor. A number of marijuana addicts when detoxing report a loss of appetite, digestion problems or cramps after eating, and nausea during the first month. Other common experiences are tremors or shaking and dizziness. Less frequent complaints include kidney pains, impotency, hormone changes or chemical imbalances, low immunity or chronic fatigue, and minor eye problems.

Unlike other drugs, THC is stored in the fat cells and takes a longer period of time to be fully discharged from the body than other drugs. Some parts of the body, particularly the brain, can retain THC for a couple of months, instead of a few days or weeks, as is the case for water-soluble drugs.

CASE STUDIES

Beginning with the publication of The Individual Delinquent *(Healy 1915), the case study method has earned distinction as a reliable method for the study of social problems and issues. The advantage of the case study is that it allows for the possibility of uncovering all the key variables related to the particular issue or problem being examined. The descriptive detail of an individual case communicates an understanding of related or similar cases. The case study can provide certain information and insights that are often not included in statistical analyses or experimental studies.*

In this context, five case studies of African Americans who used marijuana are presented. At the time of the interview, these individuals were confined to the King County Youth Detention Center in Seattle for various criminal violations. These individuals, described below, were selected because they represent a sample of males and females that reflects the backgrounds and histories that appear to be most common in the smoking of marijuana and other drugs.

> *Edward T., a seventeen-year-old African American male born in Oklahoma City in 1976, grew up in foster homes, and at age ten picked up a marijuana joint thinking it was a cigarette;*

> *James D., a seventeen-year-old African American male born in Galveston in 1976, as a young toddler was trained to walk across the room to get some alcohol on his lips and started using marijuana at age 14;*

> *Ernie S., a seventeen-year-old African American male born in Seattle in 1976, was raised in Baton Rouge and started smoking marijuana with cousins and friends at age 12;*

> *Sheliya M., an eighteen-year-old African American female born in Seattle in 1975, spent summers in Fort Worth until age ten and started to smoke marijuana and drink alcohol at age twelve; and*

> *Tamika F., a thirteen-year-old African American female, who was born in Seattle prematurely after her dad beat up her mom, started using alcohol, pills, and marijuana at age eleven.*

Together these case studies provide particular information and insights into the dynamics of marijuana use among African American youth.

Edward T.

Edward T. moved to Los Angeles when he was two years old, and when he was four to Seattle, where he currently resides. Until age four, he grew up with one brother, one sister, and his mother. He does not remember his dad but said that he hates his dad because he was told that his dad was an alcoholic and cocaine and heroin addict who had fits of violence and is currently serving time in the state

*reformatory in Monroe, Washington. His mother put him in a fos-
ter home when he was four years old, and he spent time in ten fos-
ter homes until he was adopted at age nine. He said that his mom is
a crack cocaine addict who lives in Tacoma, where he also has un-
cles who are dope dealers.*

*Edward took his first hit of marijuana at age ten, when he
picked up what he thought was a friend's cigarette. He had several
white friends whose parents were growing marijuana in the base-
ment of a neighborhood house. However, he started doing drugs
regularly when he ran away from his adoptive parents at age thirteen. He hit the streets, smoking sherms, drinking beer, and taking
LSD in beverages. At age thirteen, he recalls, he got drunk on some
Southern Comfort (whiskey) that he bought himself, after drinking
some Thunderbird (wine) that a friend gave to him.*

*At this same age, his older brother, who Edward said was his
role model, recruited him into a gang called the Gangster Disciples.
In order to "get down with the gang" he had to be initiated by de-
fending himself against fifteen gang members who were allowed to
beat him for three minutes each. He reported that making money
was the purpose of the gang, and he quickly began to sell dope. He
also continued to smoke marijuana, especially the resin, which has
a high concentration of THC. Edward reported that his older
brother was killed last Thanksgiving in a drive-by shooting.*

*He has been clean from drugs for one and one-half weeks and
is serving time in detention for stealing a gun from a friend's father.
Edward said that he has served about three and a half years in detention and could be in for about five more months. His girlfriend is
pregnant and visits him every Sunday. Edward says that he has
"started praying to the Lord for forgiveness of his sins, to protect
the baby from harm, and to watch over his family." He is working
on a high school diploma (GED) and should have it in about a year.*

James D.

*James D. is the second oldest of three children. He has two sisters,
one five years older, and the other seven years younger. All his sib-
lings were raised in the same house. James's dad was an alcoholic
and a cocaine and heroin addict who beat his mom and older sister
when James was about one year old. At this time, his mother de-*

cided to move from Galveston to Seattle with the children. It has been reported to him that one Christmas when he was learning to walk his dad and some other family members who were drunk rewarded him for taking his first steps across the room by putting alcohol on his lips. At age ten, he said, he starting getting into some trouble in Seattle when he started hanging out with gangs. His mother decided to send him to Texas during the summers to spend time with his father and his paternal grandparents. James reported that his grandfather and grandmother owned four businesses in Texas (one nightclub, a barbershop, and two barbecue stores). His grandfather was on the city council and knew the mayor. James is very close to his grandfather, who does not drink and who gave James his first job and took him to church and to father/son breakfasts. He feels that he wants to follow his grandfather in the business.

However, during the school year in Seattle James started using "weed," at about age fourteen, and began to sell drugs to get drugs. He also started using Valium, beer, gin and juice, and Hennessy, a liquor. James got his marijuana from his older sister, who smoked it and used other drugs while in an abusive relationship with her boyfriend. One night she "went off," according to James, and set her house on fire, killing her boyfriend and young son. His sister is serving time in Western State Mental Hospital.

James continued to sell drugs, including crack cocaine, to get drugs. He started using crack cocaine and sherms about once a month and said that sherms made him feel powerful and lightheaded, like he was floating on air. He had joined the Rolling Nineties Crips at about age twelve and got in the gang without any kind of initiation because his sister's boyfriend was the leader of the gang. James learned the hand signs, watched movies about gangs like Colors, and committed himself to the gang and its activities. When I asked him if he had ever been shot, he pulled up his shirt and showed me where a bullet had entered his chest within a few inches of his heart and gone out his back. He said he was shot because he had used up a two-hundred-dollar "sack" of drugs that was to be sold.

At age fourteen, he was arrested several times for selling drugs. One night, high on drugs, he was in a car with some friends when they stopped at a convenience store. He saw a woman get out of her car and leave her purse on the front seat. James got out of the car he was in, ran to the other car, grabbed the purse, and ran. The police caught him after a chase and eventually charged him with robbery. Since he had a prior record, he was sent to the detention center to serve some time.

James was born a Muslim, and his mother attends Muslim services. He has begun to read the Bible and attend church services in the detention center. He feels that now is the time to "stop and think about the life he has been leading." He had been clean from drugs for about four weeks prior to the interview and is willing to enter a sixty-day treatment center. James feels that sentences are "too light" because he said that several times he had been arrested, booked, screened, and released in the same night or by the next day.

Ernie S.

Ernie S., born in Seattle, raised in Baton Rouge until age ten, now lives in Seattle with his mother and a brother age six. His mom and dad are separated. His father comes in and out of his life and works as a doctor at a hospital in Seattle. Ernie's mom was pregnant and near delivery at the time of this interview. The father of the baby is serving time in Walla Walla Prison for assault.

At age twelve Ernie started smoking weed with cousins and friends who were about seventeen years old. At age thirteen he was hanging out with a gang called the 74 L.A. Hoovers and had a gang flag. In order to get into the gang, he reported that he had to fight a "big homie" (homeboy) to prove that he was "down with the gang" (committed to the goals and purpose of the gang). His mom and grandmother had been taking him to church with them on Sundays, but he stopped going at about age sixteen.

By age seventeen, Ernie was using sherms every day during some weeks and beginning to feel that everyone was out to get him. At this same time, he was using alcohol, beer, gin and juice, vodka, whiskey, and other liquors. Ernie was selling drugs to get drugs. He started feeling very angry and began to get into more fights and shoot-outs. In one fight at his school, he was shot and stabbed and needed thirty-two staples to close the wound. On another occasion, he was shot while on a street corner and was taken to the hospital, where doctors removed several .22 caliber bullets. Eventually, Ernie was arrested for possession and sale of crack cocaine and was sent to youth detention. He is currently working on a GED and is willing to enter a residential drug treatment program.

Sheliya M.

Sheliya M., 18, who lives in Seattle, used to spend summers in Fort Worth with her mother and grandmother. She reported that she has five brothers, three of whom she never met (they are in their thirties). Her other brothers are thirty and nineteen years old and live in Seattle. Sheliya's father is a Baptist minister who took her to church with him. He lost his home and church and used drugs, but Sheliya was reluctant to talk about how these things happened to her dad and family. She said that her dad moved to Louisiana when she was seventeen years old in order to "get his life together." Sheliya did indicate that she and her dad smoked weed and crack cocaine together.

Sheliya's first drug use was at age twelve. She was at her boyfriend's house, where she started drinking alcohol and smoking marijuana. At age thirteen, she also joined a gang called the Crips and said that she was "down with the gang" (accepted by the gang members) because she shot five girls from another gang at a shootout. During her involvement with the gang she used drugs every day until her latest arrest for possession and attempted selling of crack cocaine. She had three prior arrests for assault. Sheliya is involved in group treatment at this time in the detention center. She expects to earn a GED in about four months. Sheliya has a three-year-old daughter and at the time of this interview was two months pregnant.

Tamika F.

Tamika F., 13, was born in Seattle four months early when her dad beat up her mom. She said her dad continued to beat up her mom because he was using weed, sherms, PCP, and alcohol. At age nine she ran away from home after a fight with her mother and spent time on the street with friends, eventually joining a gang called the Bloods. Her initiation involved fighting thirty people in order to get into the gang. Each person was allowed five punches, and Tamika was hospitalized afterward for three days with three broken ribs, a broken arm, a broken leg, and a badly bruised body. Several gang members took her to the hospital.

Tamika said that it was worth the beating to get into the gang because it meant a strong bond with gang members, who will "do anything" for each other. This means they will fight for each other, kill, get drugs and money, and otherwise stick together. The gang took Tamika out to the woods so that she could have some target practice with a gun that was given to her by a gang leader. She said they wanted to make sure that she knew how to shoot and handle a gun and gave her a smaller caliber weapon that she could handle easily. Tamika also carried four small knives in her purse. Tamika said that the main rival African American gangs were the Black Gangster Disciples (the Folks) and the Crips, and she spoke about the bad feelings between these gangs, especially the Bloods and the Crips. She said that about 75 percent of all gang members are serious about their gang involvement, while about 25 percent are not serious and think that they are playing a game.

After Tamika ran away at age nine, her mother tracked her down and put her in a "receiving home" (a temporary home for runaway youth) when she was ten years old because Tamika "had become unmanageable," according to her mother. Because of this and other differences with her mother she made it very clear that she thinks that her mother does not love her.

At age eleven, Tamika started smoking marijuana, drinking alcohol, and taking amphetamines (speed), LSD, and PCP. She said she smoked weed two to three times per day and had taken about four or five trips on LSD. Tamika also smoked sherms about three times per day and said that sherms "confused her body" and made her think of doing impossible things. Tamika used drugs because she wanted to "be on her toes" all the time.

Tamika was arrested at age twelve for robbery. She described being high on LSD and PCP one night and beating up two white girls and robbing them. At the time of this interview, Tamika had been arrested three times for parole violations and served from thirty to ninety days for each violation.

Tamika feels that her generation is dying because of drugs and violence. She now feels that although the money from dealing is glamorous, you could lose your family, friends, job, home, and life. She knows many young people that have been killed or locked up for life. Tamika is pregnant, attends seventh grade at a local middle school, wants to have the baby, and has very strong feelings for her boyfriend. She said that her love for her boyfriend was so strong that if he decided he ever wanted to be with another woman, she would kill him and call the police on herself. Tamika is a recovering addict and had been clean and sober for about six months at the time of this interview. She is attending support group meetings and several rape relief classes and said that basically "gang members are looking for love."

CONCLUSION

There is a most significant lack of research on marijuana use among African Americans and a shortage of empirically validated theories that account for the observed differences associated with marijuana use between African American males and females. Studies that discuss the dimensions of the marijuana problem within tested theoretical models are much needed. There is also a need for longitudinal research to assist in determining causal, rather than correlational, factors in the origin and maintenance of marijuana use.

There is a need for longitudinal studies to assess the relationship between marijuana use and sociodemographic factors such as gender, generation, age, income, region of the country, educational background, family structure, occupation, spirituality, and cultural identity. African Americans who were raised in Mississippi during the 1950s have a cultural experience clearly different from that of African Americans who were raised in New York City during the 1950s. Also, research studies should place a greater emphasis on sociocultural factors rather than social deviance and pathology models. Research should include comparison studies on different subgroups among African Americans, using larger samples from different regions and focusing on culturally distinct patterns that shape the lives of African Americans.

5 OPIATES

It should be clear, then, that the growth of the Negro addict population has paralleled the movement of Negroes from the rural south into the urban north.

—William Bates and Betty Crowther,
  Towards a Typology of Opiate Users

African American use of opiates presents the African American community with a major challenge because the use of heroin has brought with it the related problems of addiction, violence, increased drug trafficking, prostitution, and other criminal activities. This chapter examines the history of opiate products and the involvement of African Americans in opiate addiction from historical, political, and social perspectives. The treatment of African American addicts in methadone maintenance programs is reviewed, with special attention given to positive treatment outcomes.

Since 1794, when the English succeeded in selling opium to the Chinese through the East India Company (Allen 1978), opium has been a popular and profitable drug in European and American society. Although efforts have been made to eradicate opiates from American society, the rise of narcotics dependency in the urban centers of the United States has resulted in a disproportionate number of African American opium addicts. The data on geographic distribution indicate that the problem of African American heroin addiction has its roots in urban areas, particularly in the northern cities. According to the 1960 census, nearly sixty percent of African Americans lived in the South but that same year less than five percent of the African American addicts admitted to the Lexington and Fort Worth federal prison hospitals came from that population. On the other hand, of the known addicts in treatment in these hospitals, African Americans were overrepresented at thirty percent (Bates 1968).

OPIUM

Opium is a bitter, yellowish brown, strongly addictive drug prepared from the dried juice of unripe pods of the opium poppy plant. Opium contains the alkaloids morphine, narcotine, codeine, and papaverine and is used as an anesthetic. The earliest written record of the poppy plant is Hesiod's description of the Mediterranean city of Mekone ("poppy town"), named for its extensive cultivation of poppy plants (Kritikos and Papadaki 1967). In the first century B.C., opium usage was well established in Egypt, Persia, Greece, Rome, and other Mediterranean areas. The introduction of opium into the Far East took place in the eighth century A.D., as Arab traders brought large quantities to China and India. By the seventeenth century it was well established in Europe (Anslinger and Tompkins 1953). During the eighteenth century large-scale organized trade of opium spread as Portuguese traders brought increased quantities to China. Dutch, Spanish, and British trading companies also prospered in the opium business. Eventually, the East India Company, which was operated by the British in cooperation with Chinese middlemen, established a monopoly of the Chinese trade and exported large quantities of opium grown in India (Anslinger and Tompkins 1953).

In 1805 the young German experimenter Frederich Serturner separated meconic acid from opium and produced morphine. Narcotine was isolated in France in 1817, and codeine in 1832. By this time the use of opium and its products had become fashionable in the United States and other countries. Publication of Thomas DeQuincey's *Confessions of an English Opium Eater* in 1821 had encouraged the use of opium, which DeQuincey and his followers did not actually eat but drank dissolved in sherry and flavored with herbs.

During the nineteenth century, opium products were available in the United States from physicians and over the counter in pharmacies, grocery stores, and general stores. Poppy was grown in Vermont, New Hampshire, Connecticut, Florida, Louisiana, California, Arizona, Virginia, Tennessee, South Carolina, and Georgia (Brecher 1972). Subsequently, many of these states passed legislation prohibiting the cultivation of opium, but Congress did not officially prohibit it until the Opium Poppy Control Act of 1942.

The economic benefits from the production and sale of opium were so great that in 1839 the Opium Wars broke out as a result of an unsuccessful attempt by the Chinese to prevent the British from importing opium into China. The Treaty of Nanking in 1842 legalized Chinese opium traffic to the five Chinese ports that were open to free trade. It has been estimated the United States played a role in the opium trade at this time by carrying about one-fifth of the opium delivered to the port of Shanghai on American ships. In addition, the smuggling of opium within China on American riverboats was widespread despite treaties against this kind of activity (Anslinger and Tompkins 1953).

MORPHINE

In 1806, the twenty-year-old Serturner published his report of over fifty experiments that indicated he had separated the primary active ingredient in opium. He named it morphium after Morpheus, the god of dreams. Morphine was found to be ten times more powerful than opium, and its use as a pain-killer increased tremendously with the advent of the hypodermic needle in 1853. Morphine was widely used during the American Civil War, from 1861 to 1865, the Prussian-Austrian War in 1866, and the Franco-Prussian War in 1870. The "soldiers' disease" added significantly to the number of addicts.

HEROIN

In 1874 an Englishman named Alder Wright synthesized heroin by boiling morphine and acetic acid (United Nations Department of Social Affairs 1953). After 1898, when a German pharmacologist named Heinrich Dreser investigated the potential of heroin, it became better known and available to the general public. Heroin was discovered to be about ten times more powerful than morphine and was thought to be free of the dependency-producing effects of morphine. It was touted as a miracle drug and the answer to opiate dependency. The name heroin, given to the drug in 1898 by the Bayer Pharmaceutical Company of

Eberfeld, Germany, derived from the fact that it was considered to be a heroic substance. Bayer launched a major international sales campaign to distribute the drug around the world (McCoy 1972).

In 1906 the American Medical Association (AMA) approved heroin for general use, recommending that it be substituted for morphine as a pain-killer for infections (UN Department of Social Affairs 1953). By 1910 heroin dependency was well documented. Increased use of heroin resulted in legislation and law enforcement to repress its use, but enforcement was ineffective in reducing either dependency or demand for the drug. During the early 1900s, heroin and other narcotics dependency in the United States became a major problem, with an estimated 200,000 to 400,000 people affected. Large quantities of opium were being produced in India, Turkey, Persia, Macedonia, Bulgaria, and Yugoslavia, and some of it was smuggled into the United States.

A different perspective on heroin use emerged that resulted in drug-dispensing clinics. The first legally sanctioned clinic dispensing narcotics was founded in 1912 in Jacksonville, Florida. The clinic was approved by local legislation and dispensed free prescriptions for narcotics (Musto 1973). In 1914 the Harrison Narcotic Act, enacted to put habit-forming drugs under federal control and as a revenue measure and exercise of the federal power to tax, imposed penalties for the illegal manufacture and distribution of narcotics and attempted to regulate the production, distribution, and availability of narcotics, including heroin. As interpreted by the Narcotics Division of the Treasury Department (the Bureau of Narcotics was not formed until 1930), the act stated that any doctor who used morphine maintenance to treat heroin addiction was in violation of federal law. In 1920 the Public Health Service ceased using heroin and the AMA resolved that it be eliminated from medical practice (Report on Narcotics in the U.S. 1920).

A revised form of the Harrison Narcotic Act, the Narcotic Drugs Import and Export Act, was enacted by Congress in 1922. This act authorized the importation of the quantities of opium and coca leaves that the Federal Narcotics Control Board felt were necessary to meet medical needs. Under a special amendment to this statute in 1924, the United States ended the legal manufacturing of heroin (Chambers and Brill 1973). In 1924 Congress passed legislation prohibiting the importing as well as the manufacturing of heroin (UN Department of Social Affairs 1953). The Harrison Act required registration of each dispenser of narcotics and also imposed an excise tax on narcotics. At first the Narcotics

Division was at odds with those physicians who advocated morphine maintenance as a form of treatment for addicts. Soon, however, morphine maintenance became legal for research programs focusing on experimental use of the drug. After the Harrison Act was passed, the Department of the Treasury moved to eliminate dispensers of narcotics but recommended the creation of special clinics to detoxify those who had become addicted. This was done to avoid panic among large numbers of addicted people.

The largest special clinic was opened in New York City in 1919, and additional clinics were opened in New Haven, Connecticut; Macon, Georgia; and Shreveport, Louisiana. Additional clinics were opened in California, Ohio, West Virginia, Kentucky, and Texas. New York and Connecticut had the largest facilities and represented over 50 percent of the total number of clients. From 1919 to 1923 opiates and cocaine were dispensed to addicts at forty-four outpatient narcotic clinics across the country (American Medical Association 1957). The clinics were a response to the Supreme Court decision which held that physicians in private practice could not dispense narcotics to addicts primarily to satisfy their addictions. To do so was determined to be improper professional practice and illegal under the Harrison Narcotic Act (New York Academy of Medicine, Subcommittee on Drug Addiction: Report on Drug Addiction, II, 1963).

Of the forty-four clinics or dispensaries that were established in various cities, some lasted for several weeks or months, while others continued to dispense drugs for as long as four years. The clinics generally did not require much from the clients, though the Shreveport clinic reportedly required addicts to register and obtain employment before drugs were dispensed. The clinic in New Orleans did not require registration and argued that its main goal was to protect addicts from being exploited. The clinic in New York City supplied drugs to the addict, assisted with finding employment, and provided a rehabilitation program to reduce use prior to hospitalization (Chambers and Brill 1973). These dispensing clinics typically prescribed a daily maximum of fifteen grains of morphine or heroin, decreased by a half-grain every other day until the patient felt discomfort. Then patients were offered the opportunity of complete withdrawal with some assistance or hospitalization for the remainder of the detoxification. The clinics varied greatly in their operations; recidivism rates were high and drugs were available on the streets. The clinics were forced to close in 1924, arguably due to pressure from the public and the medical profession (ibid.). Public opinion held that (1) there was no medically proven treatment for narcotics addiction, (2) death from narcotics withdrawal was exaggerated, (3) addicts would return to drugs if they were available, (4) a small number of physicians would still write prescriptions for the aged and the medically incurable, and some would write prescriptions for anyone, and (5) the clinics were just another supply source for those seeking pleasure or relief.

The concept of heroin maintenance continued to be practiced without apparent detection by some physicians in some areas of the country, and various reports, studies, and investigations continued to advocate heroin maintenance during the following decades. On the one hand, the results of the data collected over these years did not prove the effectiveness of the early morphine maintenance clinics, but neither did the data show that the clinics were a failure.

When African Americans migrated to the northern urban areas, their narcotics dependency increased. This rise in dependency was the product of environmental deprivation, individual and group alienation, deviant subculture identification, and the accessibility of narcotics (Chambers and Moffett 1970) and caused more individuals to be incarcerated in federal prisons. In response, federal officials advocated "prison farms" or "prison hospitals" for individuals affected by drugs. As a result, Public Health Service hospitals were opened in Lexington, Kentucky, and Fort Worth, Texas, in 1935 and 1938, the only public heroin treatment facilities in the United States until the 1960s. African Americans were overrepresented in the prison populations at Lexington and Fort Worth according to a review of records of 73,286 male "Negro Addict Admissions" for drug treatment to the two hospitals from 1935 through 1966 (Bates 1968). It was found that African Americans comprised nearly 30 percent of the known addicts in treatment, whereas they constituted about 10 percent of the general population.

The overrepresentation of African American addicts from a few urban areas like New York City, Washington, D.C., Philadelphia, and Chicago resulted in an overrepresentation of African Americans nationwide in the prison hospitals (Chambers and Harter 1987). African American prison hospital inmates from urban areas were primarily sentenced prisoners, although a small percentage of the inmates sought treatment voluntarily.

During 1949, the number of opiate-addicted "Negro Admissions" to the prison hospitals was more than double the number admitted in 1948, and the number again doubled in 1950 (Bates 1968). From then until 1957 African American hospital admissions were relatively stable, but in 1958 such admissions reached their highest point (Ball and Chambers 1970). From 1935 to 1945, 95.4 percent of all African Americans who entered the hospitals were sentenced prisoners. However, from 1960 through 1966, 75.3 percent of all Negro Admissions were voluntary (Bates 1968).

From 1935 to 1966, the places African American opiate addicts came from were not distributed evenly throughout the United States, as 61.9 percent of those admitted to the prison hospitals were from New York and Illinois (the states with the two largest cites in the country—New York City and Chicago). Over 90 percent of them were concentrated in nine states and in the District of Columbia, and African American addicts from New York, Illinois, the District of Columbia, Ohio, and Michigan accounted for 75 percent of the admissions. The incident of opiate addiction among African Americans residing in the southern states was low—only 10.6 percent of Negro Admissions to the two hospitals were African Americans who resided in any of the fourteen southern states. Males constituted 81.8 percent of all African American opiate addicts admitted for treatment; females made up 18.2 percent. The mean age at admission for African American males was 29.49 years, whereas females had a mean age of 28.81 years.

When America entered World War II, the international drug trade was diminished because blockades of ports and decreases in international shipping made smuggling difficult and dangerous. The street-level quantity and quality of heroin decreased significantly, the price rose dramatically, and more people went into involuntary withdrawal because they could not acquire drugs. At the end of World War II, the heroin population had decreased to about 20,000, approximately one-tenth of the number of heroin-dependent persons in the early 1900s (McCoy 1972).

After the war was over, new networks involved more importers and wholesalers in the illegal international drug traffic, making it unlikely that law enforcement efforts would have much of an impact on the drug trade. Since the 1940s, the number of "consumers" of drugs has grown enormously.

During the early 1900s heroin use was generally confined to brothels and opium parlors. The Prohibition era of the 1920s moved heroin into the speakeasies and skid row areas of American cities. The majority of drug users during these periods were European Americans and Chinese Americans. After World War II, heroin emerged in large quantities, and urban areas were targeted for distribution. More African Americans and Puerto Ricans became dependent on heroin as did European Americans from lower socioeconomic levels. The availability, low cost, and high quality of the drug made it more appealing than other drugs, and the rate of use skyrocketed as the general public ignored what many felt was a drug problem specific to ethnic minority populations.

During the 1950s, heroin became more popular among the white youth of the nation, along with youth from minority backgrounds, as they looked for a new "high." This use by more young people prompted increased publicity about the dangers of heroin, but the response of society remained inadequate and shortsighted regarding the medical, social, and economic issues involved in preventing and treating heroin dependency.

Heroin use in Harlem reached epidemic proportions in the 1950s as economic and social inducements, political and cultural exploitation, and feelings of hopelessness increased (Brown 1965). Drug dealing, now the fashionable or "hip" thing to do (ibid.), became more widespread and was accepted—or ignored—by the African American community, although punished by the police. A complex and painful world of heroin use developed that, beyond the formal laws, changed the actual fabric of society as dealing, death, crime, and fear became part of the African American urban experience in New York and other major cities.

In the 1950s and 1960s there were no inpatient hospital facilities available for drug addicts in New York and other urban areas experiencing tremendous growth in the number of heroin addicts. This lack of service in New York led to the development of methadone maintenance inpatient programs by Dr. Vincent P. Dole and Dr. Marie Nyswander at Manhattan General, Harlem Hospital, and Van Etten Hospital in the Bronx (Hentoff 1968). These programs served as models for other methadone maintenance programs across the nation.

Narcotics addiction emerged once again as a major national concern in the 1960s as the nation experienced an increase in the absolute number of addicted individuals and the drug problem spread from the urban ghettos to smaller communities and the middle and upper classes. More adolescent use, an increase in crime rates, and reports of widespread drug use by military personnel returning from the Vietnam War (described in Chapter 1) increased national awareness of the problem and led to the opening of a limited number of heroin maintenance programs.

METHADONE MAINTENANCE

Methadone hydrochloride (methadone) is an organic compound that was synthesized and used as a substitute for morphine in Germany during World War II (VanDyke 1949), when access to opium was severely limited. Methadone was subsequently used in the United States to relieve chronic pain and as a cough suppressant. The short-term medical use of methadone in treating heroin addiction and opiate-dependent patients began in the United States in the late 1940s (Vogel et al. 1948). The drug was used at the Public Hospitals in Lexington, Kentucky, and Fort Worth, Texas, for narcotics addicts. It was substituted for heroin or morphine at an appropriate dosage, then gradually reduced over seven to ten days, a procedure that produced an easier withdrawal compared to going "cold turkey."

The City of New York increased support for methadone research based on the work of Dr. Dole and Dr. Nyswander with addicts in East Harlem who were maintained on methadone at a consistent dosage level rather than being withdrawn (Dole and Nyswander 1967). Dole and Nyswander's initial hypothesis was that addicts suffer from a "metabolic disease" characterized by a "need" for narcotics in order to function normally. Evidence from several hundred patients in the Beth Israel Medical Center in New York that indicated better social adjustment, regular employment, and positive personal changes prompted rapid expansion of the program. The goals of methadone maintenance projects were to counteract heroin addiction on a large scale and to lower the rising crime rate in the urban areas.

The two largest treatment programs in the country are the Methadone Maintenance Treatment Program, which started in 1970 in New York City, and the Ambulatory Detoxification Program of the New York City Department of Health, which began in 1971 (Newman 1977). Through the end of 1974, 20,653 individuals were admitted to the New York City Methadone Treatment Program, approximately half of them African Americans; the same year, African Americans made up 60 percent of the admissions to the New York City Ambulatory Detoxification Program (ibid.). African Americans in the methadone programs were more likely to be drug abusers of heroin and cocaine and had higher rates of excessive alcohol consumption than either European American or Latino patients. Although methadone maintenance programs expanded quickly in Philadelphia, Chicago, Washington, D.C., Santa Clara, New Orleans, Boston, Albuquerque, and many other sites, there was a significant decline in the success rate reported by Dole and Nyswander. The newer clinics began to serve thousands rather than hundreds of patients, and the quality of care and personal attention for each patient was lower. This situation resulted in new regulations controlling the use of methadone and changed its status to a drug treatment that required particular minimum staff-to-patient ratios, specific patient criteria for eligibility, a basic minimum level of supportive services, and long-term studies of the effectiveness of treatment. Methadone maintenance programs are given technical assistance by the National Institute on Drug Abuse and are supposed to maintain a basic minimum standard of care. Retention in the program has been consistently viewed as a measure of success, because, it is argued, if it is assumed that methadone maintenance decreases criminal behavior and increases employment and social adjustment and that the majority of those who leave the program return to heroin use, then being retained in a program is better than dropping out.

CASE STUDY
Mrs. R.

Mrs. R., a forty-six-year-old African American, started using heroin and cocaine in the 1970s and early 1980s. At the time of this interview (in the 1990s), Mrs. R. felt that her recovery from drug use through methadone maintenance was like "being slapped in the face." She admitted a need for recovery because of a "cycle of jail, methadone maintenance, and prostitution."

Her belief in methadone maintenance is very strong, but she feels that some people "hold on to it too long," as she did. Mrs. R. said that if it had not been for methadone she would not be alive today because she would have overdosed on drugs. She said that methadone did not allow her to feel normal emotions because it dulls feelings and that methadone made it easier to use cocaine all night long because she knew methadone "would be there in the morning" as another way to lessen her emotional pain.

Mrs. R. believes that methadone is a great resource for some people who need it to get through work every day. She has friends who have been on methadone for five to ten years. On the other hand, Mrs. R. has also had friends who came off methadone but overdosed on other drugs and died. She felt that low self-esteem and self-worth are two major factors that led to drug overdoses and the death of her friends.

Mrs. R. indicated that family support was always available to her; she was always welcome at family gatherings for holidays, anniversaries, birthdays, and special celebrations, even though the family knew that she was "on the streets." Often a sister or brother would go looking for her on the streets and bring her to the family function. Mrs. R. feels that the community needs safe houses for women, particularly women on the streets who are into prostitution and drugs. She felt very unsafe on the streets. Although she wanted to quit for many years, she felt "stuck in the lifestyle."

She was still doing drugs and was "high on drugs" when she gave birth to a baby boy, whom she would often leave with friends. The father of the baby was "out of the picture" and was not very responsible. After leaving the baby in various places for almost a year of uncertain care, Mrs. R.'s family finally issued an ultimatum. Mrs. R.'s brother said he would take the baby to another sister and pay her to take care of the baby. This was the final straw that convinced Mrs. R. to begin her recovery from a life of drugs and prostitution. She went into residential treatment. After release, she rejoined her church and started regularly attending support group meetings of Narcotics Anonymous and Cocaine Anonymous. She currently works as a counselor for an HIV/AIDS prevention program and is living a drug-free life.

THE BRITISH SYSTEM

Scholars have paid some attention to the British system for managing the addiction problem in England. The system is based on the regulations related to prescriptions for opiates through the Dangerous Drug Act. This act differs from the United States Harrison Act because the British view the addiction problem primarily from a medical rather than law enforcement perspective. Under the British system, heroin and cocaine may be prescribed by doctors specially licensed by the home secretary, and it may be given for pain relief related to an organic disease or injury (Chambers and Brill 1973). The British system treats the addict as a sick person, and the medical profession is required to provide care to the addict.

THE PRESENT SITUATION

It is clear from the evidence related to methadone maintenance programs that differences in retention are based on patient characteristics. Key factors that have been identified include age, addiction history, age at which heroin use started, number of previous treatments, number of years of criminal history, patterns of drug use, and marital status. The results can be summarized as follows:

1. Older patients stay longer.

2. The longer the patient has been addicted, the longer the patient stays in treatment.

3. Patients who begin heroin use at an older age stay longer in treatment.

4. The more treatment attempts a client has tried, the better the chances in the present treatment.

5. The higher the percentage of time spent in jail during addiction, the better the treatment results.

6. The treatment results improve if the client had less involvement with drugs other than opiates.

7. Married patients, especially those with dependent children, stay in treatment longer.

Clearly, the initial expectations of Dole and Nyswander's early experiences with methadone maintenance programs have not been reached nationwide. Methadone is not a miracle drug for heroin addiction, but it can be useful as an alternative to continued heroin use. If methadone maintenance was discontinued, then the primary control of narcotics addiction would return to law enforcement officials and the number of options available to the addict would decrease. The result would be more heroin addicts becoming involved in criminal activities.

Some are advocating the legalization of heroin maintenance. It has been suggested that such maintenance would be very cheap and that pure heroin to support a daily habit would cost less than the standard methadone treatment and rehabilitation programs (Kunnes 1972). Unfortunately, methadone, originally synthesized as a replacement for morphine, is nevertheless an addictive drug. Heroin itself originally appeared as a "treatment" for opium and morphine addiction, and methadone is now supposed to "solve" heroin addiction. What is clear is that there needs to be a comprehensive treatment program that includes more than using one addictive maintenance drug to replace another addictive drug.

CONCLUSION

Carl D. Chambers and Michael Harter (1985) examined the social and psychological factors that set African American drug abusers apart from nonabusers. They found that in general four associative factors related to drug use and drug addiction have been identified consistently over several decades. Factors that have a strong relationship to narcotics addiction include dropping out of school, using marijuana at a young age, a history of addiction, and involvement in the selling of drugs. Two additional speculations about African American drug abusers that need more consideration are the relationship between drug abuse and being reared in a home where there is no positive parental figure and the relationship between drug abuse and being reared in a home where a member of the immediate family is a drug abuser. For young African American males and females it is becoming increasingly clear that the home environment—where no mother or father figure is present, a parent is emotionally distant, a parent or guardian is an addict or engaged in criminal activity or infidelity, or a parent or guardian does not provide support for the family—is strongly associated with deviant drug-using behavior.

6 COCAINE

Oh, I went to the rock to hide my face,
De rock cried out, "No hidin' place,"
Dere's no hidin' place down dere.

—"Dere's No Hidin' Place Down There"
(Anonymous Spiritual)

The crack cocaine epidemic has brought even more addiction, crime, and violence to a community that was already facing racism, unemployment, and the AIDS crisis. Can this addiction be treated? Or are its victims hopelessly addicted in the manner portrayed in so many popular movies and television shows?

Crack cocaine addiction in African American communities presents a multilayered set of problems with economic and public health consequences for many members of the community. First, there are the addicts themselves, who often exhaust personal, family, and community resources to maintain their addictions. Second, there are the distributors of the drug: midlevel dealers, gangs, "base" and "rock" house dealers, transporters, lookouts, and street dealers. Third, there are those who are responsible for addressing the crack cocaine epidemic—ministers, physicians, counselors, parents, teachers, social workers, public health officials, and community leaders. And finally, there are members of the community who simply look the other way and who deny the high price the African American community is paying because of the epidemic.

This chapter deals specifically with recovery from crack cocaine and focuses on how to assist those who are addicted to the drug and how they might achieve long-term recovery. However, first it examines in detail the development of cocaine addiction in the United States.

THE HISTORY OF COCAINE USE

Cocaine, or coca, has been used for centuries in Peru and neighboring Latin American countries. Coca leaves were chewed for stimulation, to prevent fatigue, and to limit appetite. W. Gordon Mortimer (1974), in his work *A History of Coca: The Divine Plant of the Incas,* records the history of use of the coca plant in ancient and modern Peruvian society. He also acquaints us with the Spaniard Pedro Cieza de León, the first European author to write of the coca plant. In 1550, Pedro Cieza wrote, "In most of the villages subject to the cities of Cali and Popayán they go about with small Coca leaves in their mouth, to which they apply a mixture which they carry in a calabash, made from a certain earth-like lime" (151).

The early Spanish conquerors in Bolivia quickly saw the advantages of supplying the coca leaf to the Indian slaves they worked in their silver mines, which were often as high as 17,000 feet. Each Inca village had to supply a certain number of workers, who, given the coca leaf to keep them from feeling cold, hunger, and fatigue, were literally worked to death. The population of these Inca tribes was decimated by a combination of forced labor in the mines, exposure to new diseases, and tribal genocide.

In 1565, Nicholas Monardes, a physician of the Spanish city of Seville, published the first scientific study of coca (ibid.: 153). European explorers, physicians, and scientists of this period were also curious about the role of the lime or ash that was chewed in addition to the leaf. However, an understanding of the properties of coca had to wait for the development of chemical science.

In the 1850s, European chemists were able to isolate the most active alkaloid from the coca plant and named it cocaine. In 1884, when Sigmund Freud was a young physician working in Vienna, he obtained a sample of cocaine, which he took himself. He became an advocate of cocaine as a local anesthetic and as a treatment for depression, indigestion, asthma, various neuroses, syphilis, drug addiction, and alcoholism (Maisto et al. 1991). This medical support of the drug encouraged its popularity, and the cocaine epidemic of the 1880s began. Cocaine was present in medicines and tonics frequently prescribed by physicians and was also readily available in Mariani's Coca Wine, a best-seller in Europe, and in the United States in John Styth Pemberton's Coca-Cola, which contained the ingredients called "coca," extracted from the coca leaf, and "cola" extracted from the African kola nut (Brecher 1972).

The first mention of cocaine use in American medical literature appeared in 1885, when W. Scheppegrell wrote an article entitled "The Abuse and Danger of Cocaine," published in the *Quarterly Journal of Inebriety*. Cocaine was used for eye operations, allergies such as hay fever, and some stomach ailments. In 1898, Thomas D. Crother reported that in New York City "coke" was also "available with mixed drinks or was powdered for sniffing at many big-city bars, restaurants, pool halls, and other dens" (Crother 1902: 254).

With the growth of morphine addiction among Civil War veterans, society at large became aware of a growing drug problem. As long as drugs were thought to be a problem of the Chinese, prostitutes, artists, and intellectuals, police and physicians ignored them. But use of drugs and medicine quickly outpaced population growth. Between 1880 and 1910 the national population grew about 83 percent, while the sale of patent medicines rose sevenfold. By 1882, Dr. Leslie Keeley of Illinois, perhaps one of the earliest drug treatment professionals, claimed that one in every one hundred Americans was addicted to drugs. By the mid-1880s cocaine was beginning to be widely used in American society. Use among African Americans was no different than among other groups, except that African Americans increasingly were moving into major cities, where all kinds of drug use was on the rise.

Any examination of African American drug use in the late 1800s has to take into account the growing stigmatization of drug use as a foreign, or black, or Chinese problem. Actual drug users at the time were largely white and professional. Physicians, artists, actors, women, writers, and those with medical problems comprised the largest population of addicts. The media, however, wrote of opium dens in Chinatown, drug-dealing "blacks," and Middle Eastern and European drug smugglers.

As the nineteenth century closed, cocaine was being used as a cure for morphine addiction, and many elixirs, potions, and wines contained cocaine or opium. By then American society had had a fairly lengthy exposure to morphine and opium use and was beginning to question the efficacy and safety of the two drugs. Support for cocaine use continued, however. W. Gordon Mortimer wrote in 1901:

> As to the value of Coca there cannot be the slightest doubt. As to its utter harmlessness there can be no question. . . . Medicinally employed, cocaine in appropriate dosage is a stimulant that is not only harmless, but usually phenomenally beneficial when indicated. (Mortimer 1974: xiii)

H. Wayne Morgan in his important book *Yesterday's Addicts* points out several developments in the new century that moved the country toward the stronger regulation of drug use. Among these were the widespread use of intravenous needles for the injection of drugs; the stigmatization of drug use as a practice of foreigners, Chinese, African Americans, and laborers; and the development of heroin.

In 1906 the Pure Food and Drug Act was passed to stop the abuses in the patent medicine industries. The same act eventually forced Coca-Cola to decocainize the coca leaves used in making the beverage. In 1909 opium importation was restricted, except for medical uses. In 1914 the Harrison Act, which required surveillance of all narcotic production and supervision of druggists and pharmacists, mistakenly labeled cocaine a narcotic, and since 1914 coca leaves have been controlled in the same way as heroin, morphine, and opium.

The new controls were not in place until ten to fifteen years after the Harrison Act. Cocaine use continued across the United States, and some cocaine addictions were acquired in Europe, where cocaine was still relatively cheap and available in pharmacies. Other cocaine addictions in this period showed up among individuals who were in the Merchant Marines or the Army during World War I or who participated in world travel for other reasons.

Morgan, in *Yesterday's Addicts*, states, "The Harrison Act did not end drug abuse though its enforcement probably slowed the addiction rate" (33). Passage of the act clearly reflected social alarm and made drug abuse more difficult. Morgan describes three cases of cocaine addiction in the 1920s. One man enlisted in the U.S. Army and became addicted while fighting in France. Just before coming back to the United States he bought over four ounces of cocaine in Berlin. Another individual started with intravenous morphine use and ended up addicted to both cocaine and morphine. In order to support his drug habit, this person dealt both drugs in San Francisco's Tenderloin hotel district in the 1913 to 1920 period. The third example of drug use was among several Portland youths, who began with intranasal use of cocaine and eventually injected morphine.

More extensive research will reveal more to us about cocaine use from the 1930s to the 1960s. Some researchers believe that it almost died out in this period, replaced by use of another major stimulant, amphetamines. Other researchers believe that the activity of the newly formed pharmacy boards simply moved cocaine use underground.

James Inciardi in his book *Women and Crack Cocaine* suggests that cocaine was a significant part of the 1950s African American drug scene. Present in inner-city heroin culture as the speedball, a cocaine-heroin mixture that is injected, cocaine was very much a part of the jazz world drug scene and had been so for decades. Chicago-style saxophonist Milton "Mezz" Mezzrow, who played off and on with such well-known jazz artists as Louis Armstrong, Eddie Condon, Ben Pollack, and Bud Freeman during much of the 1930s and 1940s, repeatedly mentioned in his *Really the Blues* how "jive" (music) and "jive" (heroin and cocaine) seemed to be hopelessly interwoven in life on the bandstand. Anita O'Day in her autobiography, *High Times and Hard Times,* described how she, along with so many other musicians and singers, spent much of their careers stoned on cocaine, heroin, and speed.

Cocaine, often adulterated, was irregular in supply, and very expensive. Its use in African American communities during this time occurred among individuals who had access to large amounts of money—numbers runners, pimps, club owners, and others involved in the entertainment industry.

Why did cocaine re-emerge in the 1980s as a stimulant of choice in African American communities? Did patterns of use that began in the 1960s portend a later epidemic of cocaine use?

In the 1960s and 1970s cocaine was very difficult to obtain. Stephen Maisto, in a recent book on American drug use, *Drug Use and Misuse,* claims that the difficulty of finding cocaine and the expense of the drug inhibited growth in its use in this period and that its use was limited to the movie star set, to athletes, and to criminals with money or so addicted that they committed more crimes to get the drug (Maisto et al. 1991). In the 1960s, the cost of cocaine was three to four times more than the price of equivalent amounts of heroin, which was epidemic among Puerto Rican and African American youth in the Harlem, Lower Eastside, Upper Westside, and Spanish Harlem communities of New York

City. Cocaine, on the other hand, was used by those who had ongoing access to large amounts of money and were in regular contact with members of the more affluent white community.

Most cocaine use during this period was either intranasal or intravenous. In 1978, Hollywood Henderson of the Dallas Cowboys claimed that his cocaine habit had reached $1,000 a day. Nevertheless, cocaine was still viewed as a nonaddicting drug. In 1975, Richard Ashley wrote that "cocaine was not an addictive or especially dangerous drug . . . and should be legalized" (186). Cocaine addiction was thought to be primarily a psychological phenomenon, with short-term and inconsequential withdrawal symptoms—nothing like the withdrawal symptoms of heroin addiction or alcoholism—and on this basis it was judged to be a nonaddictive drug.

Because the purity of cocaine in this period continued to be low and the drug was difficult to obtain regularly in large quantities, the truly addictive nature of the drug was not understood. Despite the many articles written on the dangers of cocaine addiction at the turn of the century, it is as if society almost had forgotten its experience with cocaine in the late 1880s and the 1890s, only to repeat it in the 1980s.

By the late 1970s and early 1980s the use of powder cocaine intranasally was becoming popular. Cocaine was more widely available to the general public, and experimentation with different methods of use was common. In California in the early 1970s, a "freebase culture" of smoking cocaine developed. Freebasing cocaine provided a more powerful "rush," and this method of use quickly became attractive to large numbers of individuals. Its use in Miami was noted as early as 1973 (Inciardi et al. 1993). With the publicity surrounding the near-death experience of comedian Richard Pryor in 1980, cocaine freebasing received national attention. It had arrived in most inner-city communities by 1978 and had reached all urban communities by 1983.

CASE STUDY
James T.

James T., a forty-year-old African American male, is currently in treatment for a cocaine addiction that started after his graduation from high school in Memphis. He states that he first became involved in alcohol use in grade school and by high school was dealing marijuana and drinking cough syrups and hard liquor. He stated

that "In 1973 in Memphis there was plenty of powder cocaine
available. I sold it to tourists, musicians, and pretty much anyone
who would buy it. It was expensive but there was plenty of it
around."

Mr. T. has also experimented with heroin and continues to use
marijuana daily or weekly. He says that his alcohol use became
very significant in 1985, that he went into treatment, and that he
has not drunk alcohol since that time. He is currently spending over
$300 per week on crack and supports his habit with money from
his employment as a laborer and theft from his employer. In the
last three years he has been drug-free for only two or three days.

COCAINE PHARMACOLOGY

Cocaine production begins in Peru and Bolivia between 1,600 and
5,000 feet above sea level. Trees that bear the coca leaf can reach a
height of twelve feet and grow only where there is a proper combination
of warmth, altitude, and wetness, such as is found on the eastern slopes
of the Andes Mountains. A typical plot or farm is about two acres with
about 14,000 coca shrubs. The first harvest takes place about four years
after planting. The coca leaves are harvested up to four times yearly and
left to dry in the sun. Coca is legal in Peru and Bolivia and has rapidly
become the leading source of income in both countries.

The dried leaves are carried to hidden labs, where they are treated
with an alkaline solution, either lime, sodium carbonate, or potash. Like
caffeine, nicotine, codeine, morphine, and heroin, cocaine is an alkaloid,
a psychoactive compound produced in each plant. The alkaline breaks
down the fourteen different alkaloids in the coca leaf, only one of which
contains cocaine. The next day the leaves are soaked in kerosene, the
dead leaves are skimmed off the mixture, and sulfuric acid is added. The
sulfuric acid interacts with the alkaloids contained within the kerosene
to produce cocaine sulfate. As the kerosene is siphoned off, more alkaline
is added to neutralize the acid. A gummy, grayish goo collects in the
bottom of the vat, and this is cocaine paste.

The paste producers in Bolivia and Peru usually sell their product to
the Colombians, who further refine the cocaine paste. Noncocaine alkaloids are removed, and other impurities are filtered out. The remainder is a very pure cocaine alkaloid called cocaine base. This base is not
soluble in water and cannot be inhaled, but it can be smoked, or free-

based. In order to create a water-soluble inhalable powder, the base is further dissolved in ether or acetone with hydrochloric acid and converted into a crystalline salt. The result is cocaine hydrochloride.

When increased production, lab capacity, and smuggling produced a glut of cocaine in Colombia, prices per kilo (2.2 pounds) were reduced. In 1982 the price of a kilo dropped from $55,000 to $13,000 (Gugliotta and Lean 1989: 113). By the mid-1980s the mass production of cocaine and its importation into the United States were well underway. From 1989 to 1992 prices of a kilo of cocaine across the United States ranged from $11,000 to $42,000. According to a 1993 report of the National Narcotics Intelligence Consumer Committee, one kilogram, diluted and sold in grams, can yield income ranging from $17,000 to $173,000. The drug suppliers make sure that money is made in these transactions. Also, the purity of cocaine varies with changes in supply, but generally the purity of a gram averaged 64 percent (U.S. Drug Enforcement Administration 1993b:17) The low price of cocaine and the large supplies of the drug have resulted in a crack cocaine epidemic across America.

CRACK COCAINE

Crack cocaine, a rocklike substance that resembles a chip of soap, is sold in pieces or rocks that range in price from $5 to $20 apiece. Sometimes it is distributed in small vials or plastic bags, but more often it is just placed in the purchaser's hand. Current estimates of the purity of crack cocaine range from 50 percent to 80 percent (the additional substances are filler materials). Drug enforcement laboratories and police laboratories report little evidence of methamphetamine or other stimulants in the crack cocaine they seize, as had once been reported.

Crack is smoked in a glass pipe or stem, which is continually relit with a lighter, matches, blowtorch, or small cotton stem soaked with 151-proof rum. When crack addicts are without a pipe they will improvise, using a broken piece of automobile antenna, foil, aluminum cans, or anything that will serve as a pipe. After the rock is smoked, a gummy substance, or caviar, is left on the pipe that users will attempt to reignite and smoke until the last hit of substance is gone. In the vast majority of users an initial hit of crack can trigger a binge that can last from four hours to one week. The compulsion to use is so strong after the initial hit that individuals will frequently empty savings accounts or sell cars, clothes, or any valuable possession in order to get more.

The two most accurate surveys of crack cocaine use in the United States indicate that approximately 50 percent of the cocaine-using population is made up of African Americans. The DAWN (Drug Abuse Warning Network) reporting system measures quarterly emergency room (ER) mentions of cocaine-related emergency episodes, which have gone from 5,000 in 1982 to over 30,000 in 1989, with an increase in deaths from 53 in 1975 to 2,332 in 1989.

In 1989, African American individuals made up 46.4 percent of total ER mentions, and in 1990, 53.5 percent. Forty-four percent of all cocaine-related deaths in 1990 happened to African Americans. Further evidence for high African American involvement in crack cocaine addiction is gained by looking at the percentage of African American populations of the top six cities with the most cocaine ER mentions. New York City had 12,633 ER mentions in 1990; Philadelphia 8,902; Chicago 4,904; Washington, D.C., 4,788; Los Angeles 4,129; and Detroit 3,888. These six cities also contain the highest African American population figures for the United States.

The National Institute of Justice Drug Use Forecasting (DUF) quarterly reports are based on quarterly urinalyses of arrestees in over seventeen major cities in the United States. The most recent DUF report focusing on race and cocaine is for the January to December 1990 period. Philadelphia and Manhattan both reported African American male arrestee cocaine use at 71 percent. African American female arrestee use was highest in Washington, D.C., San Diego, Philadelphia, Los Angeles, Cleveland, and Atlanta. African American male arrestee use was highest in Manhattan, Philadelphia, San Diego, Atlanta, Houston, Fort Lauderdale, and Los Angeles (DUF reports, 1988–1993). Philadelphia, Manhattan, and Washington, D.C., have reported arrestee rates of cocaine use ranging from 50 to 70 percent for the entire 1988 to 1993 period. These three cities are typical of addiction patterns in East Coast cities, where African American communities have been entirely transformed by cocaine addiction in just ten years. While heroin-dealing was confined to ten, twenty, or a hundred street corners, crack cocaine addiction has turned thousands of houses, abandoned cars, apartment buildings, and many other locations into places for drug dealing. The shortness of the crack cocaine high in addition to its ability to induce craving behaviors have created almost an unlimited demand for the drug. The three cities have also experienced an increase in male and female prostitution, domestic violence, and child abuse and neglect, as well as a virtual doubling of incarcerated African Americans in the last ten years. The homeless population in each city is swelled by individuals and families who have "smoked up the rent check" and who must now contend with the violence and uncertainty of street and shelter life.

When visiting drug treatment programs in these three cities one is struck by the youth of the participants. Mostly in their mid- and late-twenties, these African American and Puerto Rican young adults have spent their entire adult life in the midst of addiction. Many have a parent who is an alcoholic or addict, and most have not completed high school and have little or no formal work experience. However, along with these younger addicts a cross section of African American society is represented: grandparents who became addicted at age fifty-five or sixty, college graduates, former athletes, and individuals who had long work histories until their addictions cost them their employment.

To the trained observer, Washington, D.C., Philadelphia, and New York City are overflowing with young and old African American victims of the crack cocaine epidemic. Thin, forlorn, and in search of housing and money, such individuals are a testimony to the failures of our criminal justice and drug treatment systems. Most support their addictions with income from male and female prostitution, theft from downtown stores, drug sales, and short-term employment. In New York City and Philadelphia, African American male prostitution has greatly increased due to the crack cocaine epidemic. In New York City, male prostitutes gather in specific X-rated bookstores, in the 42nd Street and West Village communities, as well as in numerous locations throughout Brooklyn and the greater New York City area. Individuals who were interviewed spoke of numerous drug treatment experiences with immediate relapses upon program completion. Most individuals remained in contact with their parents, were homeless, and reported spending all of their daily earnings, ranging from $50 to $200, on crack cocaine.

CASE STUDY
Bernard A., from New York City

At twenty-seven years of age, Bernard A. looks hopelessly tired as he eats his pizza, payment for this interview at a 7th Avenue Italian restaurant. He reports being from Connecticut but says he rarely goes home because of his shame over his addiction. Dressed in dirty jeans and a silk T-Shirt, Bernard appears thin, yet is still muscular and attractive.

At first he denies serious cocaine use, but when I point out the burns on his fingers and lower lip he opens up about the realities of his life and addiction. He states that his addiction started at the age of seventeen and that his prostitution started about the same year. Unlike most of the males interviewed, he has never been in treatment. His only breaks from addiction have been several two-week stays in jail for prostitution.

He meets most of his customers in male X-rated bookstores and then goes to their home or hotel or to a movie room in the same establishment. He reports usually giving oral sex, but when he is really craving crack, he will involve himself in any sexual behavior. Caught in a vicious cycle of prostitution and drug sales, Bernard lives his entire life in a dangerous six-block area of Times Square.

Intelligent and yet very addicted, Bernard is visibly in cocaine withdrawal as we speak. He is shaky, irritable, and hyperactive. When asked about safe sex, he claims to be very careful about AIDS and shows me several types of condoms. Asking me for money instead of food, he asserts that he needs cash to get a room for the night. I refuse, because I believe he is lying to get money for drugs. Seeing that I am unwilling to support his habit, he quickly moves out into the night.

TREATMENT

Philadelphia has constantly been among the top American cities affected by the crack cocaine epidemic. Individuals interviewed there confirmed that crack cocaine addiction spread quickly in 1982 and 1983, when there was an apparent lack of information in the street about the addictive properties of the drug. African American youth became involved in drug sales in Philadelphia as early as 1987, with individuals from the Dominican Republic having significant involvement in inner-city drug sales.

Mark Benzavango, assistant commissioner for health in Philadelphia and responsible for the local government role in drug treatment, confirmed the large number of African Americans involved in crack cocaine addiction in the greater Philadelphia area. Like so many county drug treatment providers, Benzavango faces an out-of-control crack epidemic with few financial resources or effective organizations available to treat the victims.

Philadelphia, like other cities heavily populated by African Americans, has developed many grass-roots programs to treat addiction. Genesis II, a facility based on the traditional confrontation model of drug treatment, is located in the middle of downtown Philadelphia and enrolls both male and female participants. Participants are assigned jobs at the facility and go through levels of recovery. The main treatment focus of this residential program is a two-hour daily treatment group, as well as ongoing seminars.

Participants in the Genesis II program interviewed in 1993 seemed to be in compliance with program rules, but they lacked significant guidance in their recovery programs. Staff appeared largely untrained and constantly focused on participants' adherence to program rules rather than offering support for any meaningful spiritual or psychological growth.

The One Day at a Time program is made up of over fourteen residential brownstone "recovery houses" in North Philadelphia that house ten to fifteen residents. With a stronger spiritual focus than Genesis II, One Day at a Time focuses on empowerment of its clients and has little of the constant focus on program rules and program compliance. Members greet each other with hugs, share in cooking, cleaning, and remodeling responsibilities at each member house, and have daily encounter/support sessions. Group sessions focus on client/house relationships and past traumas that clients are working to heal. Staff at One Day at a Time lack real clinical training and group leadership skills, but still manage to have an impact on clients' lives.

Both of these Philadelphia-based programs suffer from a lack of funding for experienced staff and effective staff training. Participants in both programs attend outside Alcoholics Anonymous and Narcotics Anonymous meetings and upon reaching appropriate program levels are encouraged to work.

Crack cocaine sales in Philadelphia are diversified throughout the different inner-city neighborhoods. Philadelphia's abundance of abandoned and damaged housing makes it perfect for nighttime drug sales. More than in any other community visited, Philadelphia's drug trade lasted visibly late into the night. Prostitution related to drug use contributes to an epidemic even more resistant to treatment—AIDS.

Identifying the Addict

The disease of crack cocaine addiction creates immediate changes in physical health, appearance, personal hygiene, and individual communication styles. Weight loss, an inability to sleep, loss of sexual drive, inattention to personal hygiene, and emotional irritability are the most common physical indicators of a developing crack cocaine addiction. Other signs are an individual's loss of housing and frequent requests for loans or advances on paychecks.

Identifying individuals just beginning crack cocaine use is extremely difficult if one relies on physical appearance alone. A dramatic change in spending patterns and frequent absences from work and home are the best indicators. The initial use of crack cocaine frequently results in spending binges: an individual might use up all of his or her financial resources in one to six months. More than any other addiction, crack cocaine addiction is easily identifiable through observation of the spending patterns of the newly developing addict.

Because much of cocaine use is dependent on or triggered by the availability of money, behaviors around payday or "check days" will reveal the degree of cocaine use by the addicted individual. Initially, an individual will pay the rent and bills and then use the remainder on crack cocaine. This semiresponsible pattern of crack use, however, will most likely be maintained only as long as drug use is confined to weekends or to the days immediately following payday. Once an individual starts the daily use of cocaine, semiresponsible spending patterns will rapidly disappear.

Because the effects of crack cocaine are highly differentiated, some individuals with no family history of alcohol or drug addiction will be able to use small amounts of crack cocaine on weekends and paydays for a number of months or even years. The vast number of crack cocaine addicts move between a state of being totally out of control and a state of faking normality.

In an informal 1988 examination of over 250 case histories of crack addicts applying for Washington state-funded treatment, the most common denominator seemed to be race. Fifty-five percent were African

Americans, and 78 percent of these had a parent who was an addict. Individuals who have a family history of addiction appear to move rapidly into patterns of crack use that are entirely out of their control.

Some addicted individuals can be identified by a loss of weight, particularly noticeable in facial structure, where fatty facial deposits can disappear in a matter of days. An inattention to hygiene in a culture that places real importance on hair style, skin care, and dress can be another immediate clue to extended crack cocaine use. When an individual who has groomed carefully for weeks suddenly stops caring about his or her appearance, the cause is often a recent relapse.

In many treatment situations, clients play games of hide and seek around relapse, because they wish to avoid the consequences of relapse. Often counselors threaten clients with drug tests or program termination, and program compliance rather than the crucial issues of recovery becomes the focus. However, skilled physical observation of clients gives counselors an additional tool in determining program progress. After a counselor has worked with crack-addicted individuals for a few years, subtle behavioral and physical changes will become more obvious, and participants in treatment for reasons other than recovery will be more easily identified as needing drug dependency counseling.

One of the most frequent physical problems associated with crack cocaine use is its pulmonary complications. Symptoms reported by cocaine smokers include wheezing, black expectoration, chest pain, and back pain. Cocaine smokers are at particular risk for mediastinal emphysema (the presence of air in the mediastinum) because of the deep and prolonged inhalations of smoke. Research indicates that freebase and crack cocaine smoke is made up of 93.5 percent aerosol particulates rather than vapors. This particulate matter is deposited primarily in the peripheral regions of the respiratory tract.

Studies of the pulmonary consequences of crack cocaine use were done at Brentwood Veterans Administration Hospital as well as additional, non-VA chemical dependency programs. A total of 217 individuals were interviewed, 83 percent of whom were African American. This study confirmed that 44 percent of the study group had experienced coughing up black sputum or mucus within twelve hours of smoking, and 39 percent experienced chest pain within one hour of smoking. Twenty percent reported heart palpitations related to smoking cocaine (Khalsa 1992).

As individuals accomplish weeks of recovery, weight gain and appearance changes will be obvious. In the Cocaine Outreach and Recovery Program in Seattle, as much as twenty to forty pounds has been regained in the first two to three months of treatment. Weight gain usually continues over the next two to three years until an individual arrives at a stable level. When there is no weight gain, no improvement in physical health, and no improvement in personal appearance, the reality of any extended recovery is doubtful.

Perhaps more than any other addiction, crack cocaine affects different individuals in very different ways. Some individuals can smoke very large amounts with few physical or psychological symptoms, while other individuals may show immediate physical and psychological symptoms after initial use. Generally, with crack, as with any other addiction, a tolerance develops, and it takes more and more of the drug to get high.

It is extremely important for treatment professionals to remember not to make assumptions or generalizations about individual behaviors related to crack addiction. Statements like "all crack addicts get paranoid after smoking," or "all crack addicts can't function sexually," or "they will smoke until all the money is gone," or "they will steal all your possessions," or "they haven't hit the bottom hard enough" tend to ignore the individual behaviors that can be important considerations for helping someone into recovery. One individual can be extremely paranoid in one smoking situation and a week later be relatively at ease. Some addicts will spend all their money this month and next month somehow be able to pay the rent. Each smoking situation offers a different level of drug purity, a constantly changing brain chemistry, different smoking companions, perhaps a use of different drugs or alcohol, and different triggers that initiate use as well as an addiction that is rapidly progressing.

Psychological Aspects of Addiction

Psychological behaviors related to crack cocaine vary depending on the amount of time the individual addict has been addicted to the drug, where the addict is using the drug, and the particular progression of addictive disease in the individual. A person getting ready to get high off crack is often sweating, nervous, demanding, manipulative, and very deceptive. Once the crack is smoked the individual experiences elation, lasting from just seconds to a few minutes. This elation is extremely pleasurable and is orgasmic in its effect on an individual's body. After the initial high, many individuals move right into a deep paranoia that can involve looking out windows for police, suspicion of friends, anxiety, and panic.

For the majority of individuals this panic and paranoia subsides quickly. Within ten to thirty minutes the individual becomes obsessed with securing the next hit. Initial withdrawal from crack cocaine happens quickly and is extremely difficult. An individual feels intense, depressed, and irritable all at the same time. Until that next hit of crack is secured or the feeling of withdrawal subsides, mood swings, too, are intense and combined with an ongoing feeling of irritability.

Psychotic behavior in crack cocaine addicts is almost always found either in highly toxic individuals who have ongoing access to large or consistent amounts of crack or in individuals who have some preexisting mental health condition. Most delusions or paranoid behavior due to cocaine toxicity are situational, and individuals suffering from this problem respond well when isolated from crack use and when other medical supports are utilized. Ongoing psychotic and delusional behavior is found in some homeless, drug-dealing, and base house populations, where little sleep, poor health and nutrition, and high levels of violence contribute to a continuous agitated state. Many of these individuals, because of their contact with the drug trade, have unlimited access to supplies of crack cocaine and therefore rarely come down. They maintain a state of cocaine toxicity, or high, except when they are at the end of a binge or temporarily resting.

Much more common psychological symptoms are short-term depression, mood swings, and suicidal ideation. These post–crack use depressions and suicidal behaviors are usually related to temporary brain chemistry imbalances and can be corrected with rest, good nutrition, and abstinence from cocaine. However, some individuals who continually smoke high levels of cocaine continue to experience and report these symptoms. Such extreme emotional states develop very quickly for the newly addicted crack addict and are perhaps the most common reason for voluntary admission to treatment.

Many addicts who live in the midst of urban drug life also exhibit high levels of aggression and violence. In base houses where addicts live, deal, and use, violent arguments are fairly common over who's using too much cocaine or how someone didn't get a fair amount of crack for the money paid. Much of the violence associated with crack cocaine addiction is initiated by the gangs and street youth involved in crack dealing. Often children of crack-addicted parents, these adolescents are usually the victims of sexual and physical abuse or long-term neglect. Uncared-for by society or their parents, they exist in a world of violence, frequent incarceration, and neglect and are significantly depressed and angry.

Many individuals experience a heightened sexual libido while smoking crack cocaine. Many addicts cannot imagine smoking crack alone and almost always include in their crack use some sexual partner or situation. This partner could be an ongoing sexual partner and the drug use is incorporated into the sexual relationship. The addict could be with a different partner each time and pick up the partner at the time of drug purchase. The use of crack cocaine has actually totally transformed urban prostitution. The prostitute hustler population is now far younger, more mobile and transient, more likely to exchange sex directly for drugs rather than money, and far more vulnerable to violence, crime, and sexually transmitted diseases.

Across the United States, each city has patterns of crack addiction that are individual and unique. In some cities with large white populations, crack-addicted individuals support their drug use through sales to white customers. In other cities, prostitution is more often the way of getting drugs. The use of cocaine gives an individual a psychological sense of power and control. Manipulating others or forcing others to perform sexual favors for drugs is not an uncommon behavior among crack-addicted individuals.

For some individuals this heightened sense of sexual fantasy related to crack cocaine use is not actually carried out in the sexual situations they create or choose. For most males crack cocaine stimulates sexual fantasy but depresses sexual performance. After the crack smoking stops many individuals are left both feeling sexually frustrated and with an increased craving for more crack. However, the sexual aspects of crack addiction victimize women as well as vulnerable teenage children. It helps create a drug culture in which all people become objects and are seen as existing only to give pleasure to others.

In 1991 a study was done of the sexual behavior and crack cocaine use of fifty psychiatric patients at Bellevue Hospital's inpatient psychiatric unit, where 71 percent of the patients were African American or Latino. This study suggested that crack cocaine initially stimulated sexual fantasy in some males, but use beyond two vials quickly reduced sexual interest and performance. Females in the study reported little aphrodisiac effect from crack and an actual loss of interest in sexual activity. Many patients had a dual diagnosis, 14 percent with schizophrenia, 26 percent with mood disorders, 58 percent with personality disorders, and 2 percent showing symptoms of organic brain syndrome (Kim et al. 1992).

The last psychological trait evidenced in crack cocaine addicts is extended periods of isolation and withdrawal. Because of theft, deception, and shame related to drug use, many crack cocaine addicts live entirely outside their former circle of family and friends. Even in drug-using families, crack addicts will be more stigmatized than alcoholics and are often isolated because of their addiction. Because thefts to support drug habits are frequently from other family members and friends, the crack addict often becomes entirely isolated from support. Some crack-addicted family systems include working crack addicts who look down on "street" addicts or on those in their family who steal or prostitute for their drugs. These periods of isolation and withdrawal can last for weeks because of a misspent paycheck, small theft, or shameful event or can last for years as addicts move away from family contacts and go to other cities. Loneliness, a sense of hopelessness and bitterness, and a loss of self-esteem rapidly develop as crack addicts move deeper into their addictions.

Relapse

For treatment professionals, the high frequency of relapse is perhaps the single fact that sets crack cocaine addiction apart from other addictions. Many of the most respected inpatient treatment centers report that over 70 percent of their crack cocaine patients relapse one year after program completion. The high relapse rate of crack cocaine addicts is partially due to the wide availability of the drug, its cheap price, the lack of a variety of long-term treatment programs, and the fact that the majority of the addicts go back to the same drug-using environment they came from. However, it is our belief that the high rate of relapse among crack cocaine addicts is also due in part to the lack of attention given by the counselor and client to two factors: the role of money and sexuality in relapse.

Crack cocaine addiction is an addiction to the memories of the best experiences of using of the drug. These memories are paired with events or items that enabled the individuals to get the drug or that enhanced the actual use of the drug. Because most crack cocaine transactions involve large amounts of cash, money is overwhelmingly the strongest memory trigger related to crack cocaine use. One-month treatment programs that provide addiction education without some form of established money management after treatment offer only the fantasy of recovery to crack-addicted individuals. Crack-addicted clients who handle paychecks, cash, money orders, or tax refunds early in recovery will almost certainly relapse because of the physiological strength of money triggers. Individuals in early recovery who handle money will perspire, get an upset stomach, experience diarrhea, or get headaches because the money itself creates a visually induced memory of crack cocaine use. This memory in turn triggers physical cues that for the newly recovering addict seem almost impossible to resist. Even carrying money or checks in early recovery will cause a sort of low-level excitement that can form the basis for an eventual relapse.

Crack cocaine addicts also should avoid most sexual situations in early recovery. Because so much crack cocaine use is done in highly charged sexual situations, sex becomes paired with cocaine use. Intimacy with a sexual partner in the first months of recovery can induce strong memories of crack cocaine use experienced in a prior sexual situation and so jeopardize recovery. Many male addicts will want to continue to participate in sexual behaviors with prostitutes or women still caught up in drug life. They believe that they can participate in the sexual relationship and not use drugs. Most individuals will experientially test and retest their sexual boundaries again and again in order to discover what limits they need in order to maintain recovery.

In a recent survey of forty-five crack-addicted African American clients, 85 percent maintained that handling money and paydays were the most common triggers to relapse. Seeing the drug and sexual situations were the second and third most common reasons for relapse. Most clients will ignore the counselor's input concerning money management or sexual behaviors. These areas, entrenched parts of denial-based thinking, are rarely open to examination until the client actually has a relapse. It is only when clients are truly devastated by a relapse and are asked to examine and describe their relapses that they will begin to realize the consistent role of money and sexuality as triggers to relapse.

Crack Cocaine Addiction Compared to
Heroin Addiction and Alcoholism

A basic understanding of the similarities and differences between crack cocaine addiction and other addictions helps identify treatment issues unique to crack cocaine addiction. In treating more traditional forms of addiction such as alcoholism and intravenous cocaine and heroin use, individuals are limited in the readministration of their drug of choice by drowsiness, sickness, increasing exhaustion, or drug satiation and toxicity. A typical late-stage alcoholic will drink a dozen beers, perhaps two bottles of wine, or drink a fifth of hard liquor and go to sleep or pass out. A heroin addict will also frequently readminister the drug, but like the alcoholic will be limited in the amount by the sedative effects of the drug. In comparison, a crack addict with a habit of just a few weeks' duration can smoke crack costing hundreds of dollars in a single evening. This high ceiling of crack cocaine use is partially caused by the very short duration of the crack cocaine high. However, much of the urge for frequent readministration appears to be a perceived need on the addict's part to return to a state of chemical balance, leading addicts to binges that can wipe out housing, cars, savings, and family relationships in weeks. Addicts who do not have financial resources will sell food stamps, their clothes, and the possessions of family and friends. In many situations they will also sell their own bodies.

Crack cocaine addicts can move from early- to late-stage addictions in a matter of months instead of years. Individuals totally unprepared for a life of addiction will move into the chaos, violence, and despair of urban addictive life unaware of how it all happened. The progression of crack addiction can happen quickly on physical, spiritual, mental, and economic levels.

Physically, the addict will experience weight loss, sleep deprivation, cocaine toxicity, and pulmonary damage. Spiritually, the addict will sustain damage to self-esteem and respect, a loss of life purpose and focus, and a loss of internal controls, self-discipline, and a sense of peace. Mentally, the crack addict will have disturbed thought processes, limited short-term memory, perceived irritability, and a general inability to focus on complex tasks. Economically, the addict will spend all of his or her resources, lose long-term employment, and become temporarily unemployable.

Compared to alcoholics and heroin addicts, crack-addicted clients have much greater difficulty during early recovery. The basic difference in these addictions is the level of craving or desire to use. Alcoholics and heroin addicts experience money-based triggers, but these triggers rarely happen with the physical intensity that the crack-related triggers do. Crack addicts can experience urges at five days, or twenty days, or two months, or six months that seem totally irresistible. An individual will break out in a sweat, feel suddenly afraid, or feel very sick and then will become aware of a desire for crack. Often the physical and emotional discomfort actually precede the idea of relapse, which increases the difficulty of coping with the crack-related craving.

Many individuals are involved with cross-addiction and cocaine. The most notable example of this dual use of drugs is speedballing—using cocaine intravenously with heroin. Over 50 percent of users have real difficulty coming down from this drug mixture without the use of some depressant. The particular combination of cocaine and heroin lengthens the duration of the heroin high.

The most common drug used in conjunction with crack is alcohol, usually in the form of a couple of "forty-ouncers" of malt liquor. These forty-ouncers are actually marketed in crack-using neighborhoods, specifically to certain age groups of African American youth. Individuals who have stopped using crack without treatment or the help of a twelve-step program often increase their alcohol use. Unfortunately, most alcohol use will eventually lead the temporarily clean addict back into crack use.

Design of the Treatment Program

Designing a program for crack cocaine addicts is a challenging task. Such a program must take into account the very different learning styles that crack cocaine addicts, specifically African American crack addicts, have. Learning-style researchers have found that human beings learn in very different ways. Some of us are auditory learners, some visual learners, some kinesthetic learners, and some of us learn by what we smell or taste. Others learn by imitating or modeling another's behavior. In designing a program for crack cocaine addicts the first question is, How do these individuals learn? And the second question is, What unique ways of learning do these addicts have that are important to examine when designing their recovery program?

One observation we have made about addicts in general is that they are very observant of human emotions, mood changes, behaviors, hidden intentions, deceptions, and unspoken ideas. In order to manipulate others to get drugs, to survive in the street setting, and to determine others' actions before they act, addicts learn how to read human behavior. Crack addicts have this sense of acute observation, but they also have an out-of-proportion sense of uniqueness and specialness, a loss of control over most aspects of living, and a total lack of self-awareness and self-observation.

The life of a crack cocaine addict is a world ruled by fear. The actual experience of being in crack cocaine withdrawal is frightening enough, but to be addicted to a drug that most individuals currently do not recover from is even more frightening. Recently in a group exercise at the Cocaine Outreach and Recovery Program we asked individuals to share what it would be like to live in their shoes, with their fears. We found an almost disabling fear of relapse, of failure, of homelessness, of dying unwanted and alone. Individuals were afraid that their addictions would keep them from being parents, from ever being loved, and from ever really living.

Programs designed for the crack addict must ask, What does this individual bring to the recovery process? Is this person an African American male or an African American female? What age is he? Where is she from? What does he bring as gifts, resources, and cultural strengths that will help in designing a unique therapeutic situation that will promote his successful recovery?

Crack cocaine addicts form a culture unto themselves with a separate sexual lifestyle, secrets, behaviors, and language. The chemical dependency counselor has to understand the language of addicted group members: a "cluck" is an individual addicted to crack, a "strawberry" is a woman exchanging sex for crack, a "double up" is getting twice the amount of dope because the addict is getting a larger quantity, a "raspberry" is a male exchanging sex for crack, a "base house" is a place where people buy crack and smoke it until they run out of money, a "straight shooter" is a glass stem used to smoke crack, and "geeking" is being afraid immediately after smoking crack.

Our particular assumptions about crack cocaine recovery encourage us to place an early emphasis on participant honesty. African American culture stigmatizes individuals who are not for real, who are phony or appear to be inauthentic. Because we assume that most recovering individuals will have early relapses, we suggest that the initial program focus on honesty rather than recovery. We advocate communicating clearly that we are more interested in authenticity than performance and that recovery starts when one is able to communicate honestly about one's self-destructive behaviors. We advocate program designs that have no negative consequences for relapse but that allow clients to move into intensive relapse prevention phases.

By communicating that we are not interested in a compliant client or an adaptive client but rather a client who struggles to present an increasingly real picture of himself or herself, we lay down different ground rules for recovery. Our belief is that African American clients in particular do not respond well to compliance-focused situations. Our particular emphasis on honesty is mostly informed by observing behaviors in traditional recovery programs. In most treatment situations addicts simply perform, become treatment smart, and say the right things. Many actually want recovery badly, but the compliance-based program limits any real authentic behavior or truthful connection with other human beings.

Because our recovery work is with African American individuals whose concept of individual identity is highly defined by group membership, we place the second emphasis in our program on group bonding. Our belief is that clients need new information, but they also need to know that someone else cares to know what it is like to be them. Addicts can be given prerelapse training, know about triggers, and have early recovery boundaries, but if they are still essentially isolated and alone the emotional pressure of that loneliness will become unbearable. The settings, the time length, the place of therapy, and how safe it feels to the client are all determinants of levels of client recovery.

In crack cocaine recovery there are very important pieces of information the newly recovering addict must first understand and then begin to practice. The therapeutic group is therefore a place of addictive disease education, a place of understanding, a place of bonding, and a place of self-discovery.

Many programs subscribe to a treatment philosophy that avoids issues of emotion or pain early in recovery. Our own particular approach is to address these issues in the safety of intensive outpatient groups as those subjects come up in the natural progression of therapeutic work. When we enter into an area of emotional trauma that participants are not yet ready to explore we let them know it is all right to deal with emotional healing step by step. We do not push clients or confront clients; rather we attempt to provide a safe setting in which clients can address necessary trauma issues in their own time.

Our approach focuses on telling one's story as an essential component of self-healing. This process of storytelling connects each member of the group. Group bonding is a specific therapeutic goal. The counselor also uses the group setting to pursue addiction education goals.

There are three levels of culturally appropriate treatment. First, clients should work with counselors who look like them, speak their language, and have had similar experiences and issues. Second, counselors should analyze the learning style of the client and determine the ways in which the client can receive the necessary recovery information. Third, the design of programs should be informed by the particular experience of oppression and racism a cultural group has had in relationship to majority American culture.

Our assumption about addiction is that it is a disease of dependency that happens in specific cultures where alienation, human suffering, personal brokenness, and greed are at a maximum. Drug epidemics often happen at cultural transition points, when a particular culture is at a point of vulnerability. Each particular race, racial subgroup, or cultural group has specific suffering related to its addictions that have to be addressed in order for recovery to continue. It is essential that gay and lesbian individuals in recovery be given chances to talk about their addictions in relation to the loss of their friends to AIDS. African American men must talk about their addiction in relation to racism in employment, or fears of failure, or feelings about their own parents, especially their fathers.

African American populations in recovery need to learn in different ways than the majority group culture (Williams 1992). As crack-using African Americans are actually a subcultural group of African American people, our belief is that there are multiple factors that affect learning styles in this population.

Many drug programs that focus on blackboard and video (conceptual and auditory) learning will fail because of the inability of crack-affected clients early in recovery to focus on and process conceptual information. Not unlike that of crack-affected children, the attention span of newly recovering clients is of very short duration, and rarely are they ready for sustained lectures or video presentations. Many African American crack-addicted clients will have very narrow learning styles or depend on one style of learning new behaviors. In the African American clients we have seen, the most common learning style is a visual one based on modeling and imitation. Building into recovery programs the opportunity for learning situations that stress modeling behavior will significantly increase the transmission of effective recovery information.

Sadly, most current recovery programs for crack-using African American populations replicate programs that appear to work in the majority culture. We suggest a learning approach that is relationship-focused rather than information-focused as most effective for the African American crack-using populations. The emphasis is not on getting the right information but on group membership, group loyalty, and group identification. Information necessary for recovery is constantly transmitted through the group process, rather than via independent lectures or video presentations.

African American culture places a high value on being well spoken and courageous, on honest confrontation and communication. The therapeutic group offers a place of healing for individuals who in addiction have lost their ability to speak up, speak out, and speak clearly about the dilemma of their crack addiction. Traditional lecture and video presentations focus on information rather than people and lose their utility for crack-addicted clients searching for validation, meaning, and healing.

What the recovering crack-addicted African American needs most, however, is new information about how to maintain long-term recovery. He or she must learn what triggers his or her relapses, about sexual- and money-based triggers, and about the entire process of denial and relapse prevention. Our belief is that this information will be best internalized if it is taught within the group.

Because of their experience with sexism, racism, or abuse, specific groups of African American crack addicts have specific recovery needs. Well over 50 percent of crack-addicted African American women experience sexual abuse. Males traditionally have experienced traumatic physical abuse at the hands of police, parents, or other addicts. Healing from racism, incest, physical trauma, and oppression is a significant part of the recovery task and should not be avoided by believing that every addict is the same.

Eliminating the most significant trigger for relapse—the stimulus of money, cash, and paychecks—early in the recovery process will improve the individual's chance of recovery by over 50 percent. Educating clients about the significance of money triggers is best done after a significant relapse when the client has spent his or her entire paycheck on a cocaine relapse. Money management should be offered in such situations not as a requirement, but as an opportunity for the client to salvage what is left of his employment, relationships, and property. For the client recovering from extreme addiction, education about money and relapse is best accomplished in group settings where the link between relapse and the handling of money is clearly established.

The second stimulus or trigger for crack use is sexual fantasies, behaviors, and situations. Because for many individuals sexual behavior and crack cocaine use are linked behaviors, these clients will need to be educated about how to avoid sexual situations that can reignite drug craving and use.

Often ending extended cocaine use is much easier than leaving sexual dependencies where the sexual relationship offers the rush that cocaine used to bring. The majority of nonmarried clients in crack recovery programs move immediately into dependent sexual relationships after stopping crack cocaine use. Such relationships offer a sort of security and stimulus but significantly increase the risk of relapse. The newly recovering crack client can quickly create within a dependent sexual relationship the same insanity that existed in his or her life of addiction. Encouraging clients to limit their relationships to friendships in the early months of recovery will greatly improve clients' chances at long-term recovery.

Individuals in early recovery from crack cocaine addiction are very vulnerable to renewed cocaine use based upon continued exposure to loved ones who are addicts, community gang members and dealers, and drug-related retail stores. Most addicts will have to avoid loved ones who still continue to smoke crack in order to stop themselves. The knowledge that the cousin downstairs has crack in his pocket he's going out to sell or that the husband is upstairs smoking negatively stimulates the individual in early recovery.

Many women are dependent on the drug earnings of their boyfriends and will have to find housing and alternative incomes, as well as deal with the loss of their most significant relationship. Individuals in transitions like this are vulnerable because nothing is stable. The separation between those who continue cocaine use and the recovering addict is essential and should not be ignored or discounted because of the difficulty involved.

For many individuals, old drug-using areas will have great significance. Recovering individuals will not drive by old drug houses for months until the locations lose their ability to restimulate the desire for cocaine. Crack cocaine use is paired with the memories of its use, and so old friends, houses, street corners, sexual relationships, and, of course, the actual drug will stimulate cravings.

During our treatment program we inform clients that they should anticipate experiencing irresistible urges in the first year of recovery. We teach that most irresistible urges are ignited by exposure to a stimulus or trigger unique to the addicted person. Preventing relapse is based on developing a knowledge of personal triggers and not having immediate access to money when these triggers are activated.

CASE STUDIES

Mary A.

Mary A. is a thirty-year-old African American woman with a cocaine addiction of two years. She lived with her grandmother until her recent marriage and has smoked cocaine daily or weekly since that time. She has a two-year-old child, is currently pregnant, and is seeking treatment for the first time.

Mary is married to a twenty-eight-year-old African American male who has drug-dealing brothers and sisters. Mary must leave her new husband and friends to protect her unborn child and gain recovery for herself. Without relatives who can help her, she has no place to go. Government programs will give her housing but cannot take her with her two-year-old child.

Early in treatment Mary tried to live with her husband but realized that her environment contained too many triggers. She now lives in a motel, attends church and daily outpatient groups and Alcoholics Anonymous and Narcotics Anonymous meetings, and is looking for housing. To accomplish these few months of recovery she has had to leave her home, friends, and family.

George T.

George T. has been in treatment for ten months and at first never thought he could accomplish recovery. A thirty-year-old African American male, George lived directly across from some gang mem-

bers who gave him credit for crack, which he would repay on his bimonthly payday. He has three children and a wife who also smokes. Frequently relapsing in his first two months of recovery, George moved to a friend's house, attended a men's retreat, and started attending daily AA meetings before work. Now he is able to live at home because he has completed several months of recovery and he finds the people and events that used to trigger his relapses now have little effect on him.

Mikey S.

Mikey S. was raised in a family in which his mother sold drugs for a living. One key to this forty-year-old's five-year recovery from crack was cutting the ties with friends and relatives who still use. Separated from his mother by illness and from the city of his birth because he was wanted by the police, Mikey found himself in an entirely new environment where he had a real chance to get well. Although his brother moved also, Mikey decided he would not talk to or be around him while he was still addicted. When friends relapsed he maintained firm boundaries with them.

Attending daily NA and AA meetings for the first year, as well as church services and outpatient care, Mikey S. has worked the entire time in a restaurant, where he has moved up from cook's helper to kitchen manager. Taking care to never be around people who smoke cocaine, and to always be around those in recovery, Mikey S. offers real leadership to others who want recovery.

CONCLUSION

After working daily with crack cocaine addicts for roughly a decade, we remain deeply alarmed about the impact of crack addiction on African American and other communities. Recovery from the drug is still rare, and relapse common. A generous estimate would have one crack-addicted person out of ten quitting on his or her own, one quitting because of a twelve-step recovery and treatment program, and the other eight out of ten continuing their addiction.

The very core of problems in inner-city America is the high relapse rate in crack cocaine addiction. This relapse rate results in the homeless remaining homeless, criminals repeatedly being arrested and jailed, and children continually experiencing a living hell. Crack cocaine addiction must be understood as a chronic serious illness that, like diabetes, asthma, cancer, or a heart problem, requires ongoing support, education, and care. Treatment of one month, three months, or even one or two years will not automatically result in sobriety. Having a chronic illness, crack-addicted individuals need consistent community-based care more than they need long-term intensive care.

The crack cocaine epidemic in African American communities has expanded well beyond the ability of the government to control or treat those involved. Recovery of the African American community from the crack cocaine epidemic is entirely dependent on communities generating their own programs, solutions, and grass-roots approaches. Governments on the local and national level have abandoned inner-city communities to the crack cocaine epidemic and to the accompanying violence and crime. Inner-city violence and gangs are generated by the crack cocaine epidemic. No ongoing police solution to the problems of inner-city violence will exist until we begin to successfully turn the tide of inner-city addiction.

7 GANGS

Two or more persons engaged in antisocial behavior and who form an allegiance for a common criminal purpose and who individually or collectively create an atmosphere of fear and intimidation within a community.

—Definition of a gang
  (Louis Gonzales 1993)

Gangs in America developed from a long tradition of group violence. From 1760 to 1900, about 500 vigilante groups were active in this country, including the Ku Klux Klan and the White Cappers (Gurr 1989). Lynch mobs were responsible for murdering 3,000 to 4,000 African Americans between 1882 and 1951 (ibid.). Generally, gangs were formed by young men with either racist attitudes toward ethnic and religious minorities or shared feelings of frustration about restricted economic opportunities and resentment of social systems. Some gangs were glamorized, such as Butch Cassidy's High Five and the Jesse James gang.

In the early 1900s, adolescent gangs began to emerge. Frederich Thrasher's seminal research (1927/1963) of 1,313 gangs in the Chicago area described how a play group can evolve into delinquent gangs:

It does not become a gang . . . until it begins to excite disapproval and opposition. It discovers a rival or an enemy in the gang in the next block; its baseball or football team is pitted against some other team; parents or neighbors look upon it with suspicion or hostility . . . the storekeeper or the cops begin to give it shags (chase it); or

some representative of the community steps in and tries to break it
up. This is the real beginning of the gang, for now it starts to draw
itself more closely together. It becomes a conflict group. (26)

The study by Thrasher focused on concerns that continue to be relevant
in contemporary discussions about gangs: the reasons for gang formation, the process of gang formation, situational gang leadership, personal rewards from gang involvement, the influence of family and community, groupthink, and gang rivalries. Other researchers such as
R. Lincoln Keiser (1969) and John Hagedorn and Perry Macon (1988)
have described gangs in Chicago in more detail, and Alex Kotlowitz
(1991) provides intimate stories and insights into some of the main
African American gang groupings: the Vice Lords, the Disciples (now
known as the Black Gangster Disciples or The Folks), the El Rukns (for-
merly known as the Blackstone Rangers), and the Nation.

   Robert Edgerton offers a comprehensive view of the factors that
contribute to gang formation and proposes that the major factors
include:

> . . . residential segregation in low-income areas, poverty, poor
> school performance, little parental supervision, discrimination, and
> distrust of law enforcement. In these conditions, young people
> spent much of their lives together on the street where a gang
> served them . . . as surrogate family, school, and police. We also
> hear from gang members . . . about the appeal that gang mem-
> bership has for them—friendship, pride, prestige, belongingness,
> identity, self-esteem, and a desire to emulate their uncles and older
> brothers who were gang members before them. (1992: x)

The study provides additional information on what gangs are, who com-
prises them, what they do, how they function, and how they are perceived by the community.

   According to Tully S. Lale (1992), gangs have their own hierarchy
that consists of hard-core leaders and members, regular members,
"wanna-be's," "fringe/claimers," and "could-be's." The hard-cores are
typically the leaders of the gang and comprise about 5 to 10 percent of
it. Generally, these hard-core leaders have been in the gang longer than
others, have been in and out of jail, and are familiar with some legal
matters. Often unemployed, they typically use and are involved in the
distribution of drugs. Their average age is early- to mid-twenties, and

they set the agenda and priorities for the gang. The regular members, who are mostly between fourteen and seventeen years of age, tend to support the hard-core gang members; if they remain in the gang, they are likely to become the next generation of "hard-core" leaders.

The wanna-be's are not officially members of the gang but act as though they are and hang around the gang trying to achieve status and membership through acts of daring. For example, they might seek recognition by writing the graffiti of the gang. The average age of the wanna-be's is eleven to thirteen years of age. Fringe/claimers are not members but "claim" to be members in order to feel protected in the neighborhood. They are generally in and out of the gang's activities and may be in for partying but out for committing criminal activity. They are usually between the ages of eleven to eighteen and are sometimes at risk for harm by being in the wrong place at the wrong time. Could-be's are of elementary school age and live in or nearby neighborhoods where there is gang activity. They may have a family member or friend involved in the gang, and they are potential gang members unless alternative activities are available that preclude gang membership.

AFRICAN AMERICAN GANGS AND DRUGS

In the 1960s and 1970s gangs protected turf-based territories through the use of violence; the 1980s and 1990s brought more involvement in the drug market. Factors such as unemployment, single parenthood among young females, the need for a sense of belonging and acceptance, and the lure of large amounts of fast money have contributed to the increased numbers of African American youth joining gangs.

Ronald Huff (1990) defined gangs as having three different motivational categories: scavenger, territorial, and corporate. Generally, the members of scavenger gangs share a strong need to belong and act impulsively. For example, scavenger gangs prey on others through senseless and spontaneous acts of violence. Leadership in these types of gangs changes regularly because the gang does not have a particular purpose. It is reported that the members of these gangs are generally from the lower class and the underclass and are low achievers, often illiterates with short attention spans who are prone to violent, compulsive behavior (ibid.). However, our interviews with African Americans involved in gangs (see Chapter 4) indicate that gang members are smart and articulate in expressing their issues.

Territorial gangs have leaders and designate certain things, places, or persons as belonging exclusively to the gang. The territorial gang defends and controls the defined territory, such as the street corner or the drug house. They protect their particular business and punish those who interfere with it. Corporate gangs are well organized, with strong leaders, and make illegal money-making ventures their main goal. Promotion within the gang is based on merit, discipline, and understanding of the role of gang member (ibid.). These gangs are generally organized around racial or multiracial structures.

Research findings indicate that in urban African American communities the high rate of crime is related to gang activities, to alcohol and other drug use, and to drug networks (De La Rosa, Lambert, and Gropper 1990; Dembo et al. 1990; Glick and Moore 1990; Hamid 1990; Spunt et al. 1990). Estimates suggest that more than half of all gang members are African American (Spergel et al. 1989). This estimate may reflect a disproportionate focus by law enforcement officials on African American youth and underestimate the number of white youth involved in gangs, but it does reveal a serious problem with gangs, drugs, and crime in African American communities in the United States. The leading cause of death among African American youth is homicide, at a rate seven to eight times higher than that of white males (Roper 1991).

We have no precise written history of how African American involvement in gangs began. However, according to the stories that have been passed down, it goes back to social clubs formed in the late 1950s and early 1960s in Los Angeles—the Businessmen, the Slausons, the Black Cobras, the Gladiators, and the Boozies. These young African American men hung out, took pride in their dress, cars, and women, and banded together for parties and for protection from guys from the other clubs (Bing 1991). The fighting that occurred was one-to-one combat with fists and occasional weapons like chains, tire irons, and bumper jacks.

The Watts riots broke out in 1965 and from the ashes sprang the militant African American political organizations such as the Black Panthers and US. These organizations attempted to provide African American youngsters with a sense of pride and unity, but many of the youths did not want to align themselves politically or philosophically with the organizations of Elijah Mohammed, Malcolm X, or Martin Luther King, Jr., because they did not share their religious beliefs, nonviolent philosophies, or need for commitment to a certain program or plan of action.

One story has it that in 1968 or 1969 a group of African American males organized a gang at Fremont High School in Watts. At the same time the block club concept of neighborhoods protecting themselves against property crimes and violence was being encouraged. A large percentage of residents in the Watts area were older Japanese Americans who spoke fractured English. The police recommended that they travel in groups in the area and, if attacked, yell and wave their hands to attract attention and help. One night a group of these folks were walking to catch the bus on Central Avenue when the Fremont High School gang suddenly came bearing down on them. The elders did what they had been told to do: yell and make a lot of noise. As a result, the kids grabbed a few purses and ran off and the police quickly arrived on the scene. When the police asked for a description of the assailants, a lady in the group said one of the kids was "a crip with a stick," by which she meant a boy with a bad leg who was carrying a cane. A police reporter who was hanging around the area that night picked up on that word, *crip*, and the gang had its name.

The Crips continued to intimidate others, including other youths. In the city of Compton, a group of youngsters formed the West Side Crips and took on an association with the color blue, from the blue-and-white bandannas they used to cover their faces during their "missions." Soon other African American youth felt they needed to organize so they could stand up to the Crips. The Piru Street gang was formed to oppose the Crips. They took up the color red, from the red-and-white railroad bandannas they used, and began to call themselves "Bloods," a name that African American soldiers in Vietnam had applied to themselves.

The low-income housing projects were the spawning grounds for the early Crip and Blood sets (Bing 1991). Soon, gang sets such as the Grape Street Watts (Crips), the Imperial Courts Crips, the Bounty Hunters (Bloods), the Alley Bishops (Bloods), and the Block Bishops (Bloods) began to pull together. The sets continued to multiply—the Kitchen Crips, the Outlaw Crips, and then the Hoover Crips, covering the blocks from Forty-third to 112th streets between Hoover Boulevard and Budlong. On the other side of the freeway, the Rollin' Sixties took control of the streets that "roll" up from Fifty-second Street through Tenth Avenue and areas west and east.

During this time the Crips outnumbered the Bloods by about seven to one (ibid.). The first conflicts between Crip factions were typically small fights, but in the early 1970s, when a member of the Rollin' Sixties and a member from Hoover got into a fight over a girl, there was a killing that led to lengthy conflict as other Crip sets took sides. Conflicts between Crip sets and other gang factions broke out throughout the 1970s, 1980s, and 1990s. According to Leon Bing (1991) there are forty-three known Blood sets and fifty-six Crip sets in Los Angeles which claim memberships that range from twenty African American youth to over one thousand. A gang set that is considered to be "deep" has about three hundred members.

The older members of these gangs who have made reputations for themselves and remain affiliated with the gang in some manner, such as through drug dealing, are called OG's, or Original Gangsters. According to Sanyika Shakur (1993), Original Gangsters have to go through three stages of making a reputation in order to earn the title: first, they must build the reputation of their own names; second, they must build an association between their own names and a set so that when their names are spoken the set's name is spoken of in the same breath; and third, they must establish themselves as promoters of Crips or Bloods, depending on which side of the blue/red color bar they live.

In Los Angeles County, an estimated seventy-thousand young people are affiliated with seven hundred gangs ethnically dominated by Mexican Americans and African Americans. It is also estimated that 90 to 95 percent of the young people in Los Angeles County are not members of gangs (*Gangs, Cops, and Drugs*, an NBC news special, hosted by Tom Brokaw, August 15 and 16, 1989). Most members of the African American gangs in the county, which tend to be territorial, are associated with the Bloods or the Crips. These supergangs also operate in other parts of California and in other states. Law enforcement officials estimate that about ten thousand of the county's gang members, or about one in seven, are involved in the drug trade. The number of gang members involved in violence varies widely from district to district.

Mario De La Rosa and F. I. Soriano (1992) included a sample of African American youth in a larger study of youth between the ages of fourteen and seventeen who had been seriously involved in criminal behavior and were from the Miami–Dade County geographic area. Serious involvement in criminal behavior was defined as having committed a total of either ten or more felonies or one hundred or more misdemeanor crimes over the past twelve months. Data on participants in the study were collected over an eighteen-month period spanning 1986 to 1987, with each interview lasting an average of forty-five minutes. The interview consisted of a questionnaire that elicited information on social status, family composition, school performance, criminal activities, and drug use. Interviews were conducted in homes, in the streets, in bars, parks, and social clubs, and in other places where the youth could be found.

The Miami–Dade County area of Florida was chosen because it is a large urban area—it had a population of 1.6 million in 1990 and ranked twenty-first in size among major urban areas. It also had the highest crime rate of any urban area in the country, almost twice that of the entire United States (U.S. Department of Justice 1990). The Miami area is also known as a major drug use area and an import center for illegal drugs, in particular cocaine and opiates.

Of the 198 African American youth involved in the study, 49 (25 percent) were female. The mean age of the group was 15.6 years. The data on the African American sample indicated that males and females were more likely to come from families where a female was the head of household (72.9 percent) and the main source of income was welfare benefits. The African American youths were less likely to have family members who were high school graduates (37.6 percent) or were employed. African American females had the lowest mean number of years of school completed (8.7 years), followed by African American males (9.0 years), who were more often expelled or suspended from school (89 percent) than other Miami–Dade County youth studied.

When asked which two crimes produced the most income, 69.1 percent of African American males indicated participation in the drug business and stolen goods offenses. The majority of African American females (83.7 percent) cited prostitution as the crime bringing in the most money, followed by the selling of drugs (52.9 percent). Sixty-four percent of the African American males carried handguns with them when committing crimes, compared to 20.4 percent of African American females.

Information obtained on drug use patterns indicated that African American females preferred alcohol to other drugs at a much higher rate than African American males. African American females were more likely to have tried cocaine powder, crack cocaine, or cocaine paste and to have tried it at an earlier age than African American males. Cocaine powder was indicated as very popular among African American males: 98.7 percent had been regular users at one time. In general, cocaine

powder and crack cocaine were the two most popular cocaine substances; 56.4 percent of African American males and 46.9 percent of
African American females were daily or regular (three or more times per
week) users of cocaine powder, and 69 percent of African males and
females were daily or regular users of crack cocaine.

These findings on African American patterns of drug use and criminal activity are disturbing because the youth were involved in a range
of gang-related criminal activity that included major felonies, robbery,
assault, burglary, motor vehicle theft, petty property crime, shoplifting,
theft from vehicles, pickpocketing, prostitute theft, confidence games,
forgeries, stolen goods offenses, property destruction, vice offenses, prostitution, and the drug business. Only a combined 12 percent of African
American males and females indicated having participated in substance
abuse treatment.

Terry Williams (1989), a sociologist and "urban ethnographer,"
studied a corporate drug gang in New York City for five years, from
1982 to 1986. He found that retail distribution and sale of cocaine in
New York City are controlled by Latino and African American gang
members under eighteen years of age. Williams spent time each week
with the eight members of a teenage cocaine ring, "The Cocaine Kids,"
all of whom were young adolescents between the ages of fourteen and
sixteen. Williams hung out with them and documented their movements in the streets, in homes and apartments, and in cocaine bars,
after-hours clubs, discos, restaurants, and crack houses. Seven of the
eight gang members were from the Dominican Republic. They sold
drugs wholesale to other dealers and retail to users. The source of their
drug supply was referred to only as the "connect," or connection. Only
the leader of the gang knew who "the connect" was or had contact with
this individual. Only he had the ability to speak Spanish with "the connect," a Colombian.

CASE STUDY
Mr. C.

*Mr. C. is an African American in recovery from drug addiction who
was involved in drug use and dealing for gang members in Portland,
Oregon, in the 1980s. The following interview took place on April
16, 1993, in Seattle, Washington.*
    The first thing to realize about these gangs is that they were

not just a few kids with a couple of kilos of cocaine. These gangs were organized, well thought-out, very violent, and security conscious. When they first moved into Portland, they would find welfare mothers, retired individuals, anyone in their own house or apartment who really needed additional funds and who would sell crack for them. A little later they would have the money to rent a house and then they would set up a "base house" or "rock house" in one of Portland's neighborhoods.

Mr. C.:

The fellows I worked for were from the Los Angeles area. They kept most of their drugs in a nice suburban house outside of Portland along with their earnings. They would bring crack into downtown Portland every day or so to resupply us. We sold a lot of crack every twenty-four-hour period. On the first of the month, called "Mothers Day," we would sell three or four times what we normally would sell in a twenty-four-hour period.

[At the end of each month one of the California gang members would drive back to L.A. with the gang's profits and return before the first with the new supply of drugs.]

I got to know these fellows pretty good. I believe some of them were wanted for murder in California. I was about thirty-six then, so compared to me they were just kids. Some were just seventeen or eighteen. I believe the oldest couldn't have been over twenty-three.

In the particular house I ran we would let people in to smoke till they ran out of money and then kick them out. Some houses just sold dope. You could never even get inside. Eventually one month I smoked most of the cocaine that I suppose to sell. I knew I was in deep trouble with these kids so I went into hiding. They eventually found the house I was hiding in, and searched it from top to bottom. I was in the back of a closet for I had seen these same fellows almost murder a couple of people for far less than I had done.

I'll never forget when this one gang member pulled back these clothes above me in the closet and looked dead in my eyes. I was sure he saw me, but he yelled out to the other fellows, "He's not in here." Right till this day I believe God blinded him to give me a second chance. Within a few days I was in Seattle, the city I have found recovery in.

These California gang members I sold dope for all went to jail
with federal cases. I mean they're probably all doing twenty- to
thirty-year terms right now in federal prisons.

AFRICAN AMERICAN FAMILIES AND DELINQUENCY

Over the past sixty years, the African American family has been at the center of public controversy, portrayed as highly disorganized and disintegrating. E. Franklin Frazier (1932, 1934, 1939) and Patrick D. Moynihan (1965, 1967) described the African American family as rife with social pathology.

Factors such as family instability and the lack of supervision and guidance, appropriate role models, employment opportunities, and meaningful adult relationships may be factors that explain the appeal of gangs to African American youth and their subsequent involvement in delinquent behavior. Waln Brown (1978) stressed that joining a gang is an elementary survival technique. He argues that gangs teach African American youth the lifestyle needed to function safely and efficiently in the ghetto. The early exposure to street life in the ghetto leads many African American youth to join gangs, which in turn become an extended family.

Researchers studying arrests and delinquency in two generations of African American families and their children in St. Louis, Missouri, found that the rate of delinquency for boys was 31 percent, with very little change in delinquency rates over a generation in the same cohort (Robins et al. 1975). Parental arrests (juvenile and adult) were an extremely potent predictor of children's arrests, for girls as well as boys. This is an important finding, as it has been quite commonly thought that delinquency was mainly influenced by peer groups.

In a study seeking ways to identify youths at high risk for future drug use, delinquency, or criminal behavior, 399 youth who were detainees at a regional detention center in the Tampa Bay area were interviewed (Dembo et al. 1990). Their average age was sixteen. Most of the youth were reinterviewed eleven to fourteen months later. Of the 298 youths still involved in the study, 42 percent were African American.

When compared with white males, African American males reported less physical abuse and less alcohol use both preceding their initial interviews and during the follow-up period, and they showed a higher level of emotional/psychological functioning at the initial interview. Among females, African Americans reported less alcohol use prior to their initial interviews and they had a higher level of emotional/psychological functioning when measured during their follow-up interviews. For African American youth, a significant, positive relationship existed between physical abuse and lifetime frequency of marijuana/hashish use.

The study recommended a comprehensive screening of youth entering the juvenile justice system to identify problems in four major areas: (1) emotional/psychological functioning, (2) experience of physical abuse, (3) experience of sexual victimization, and (4) alcohol and other drug use. In addition, the study recommended that additional research focus on the importance of staff training for those working with high-risk youth, early intervention efforts for youth with multiple problems, and evaluation of the impact of long-term interventions for seriously troubled juveniles.

AFRICAN AMERICAN JUVENILES AND VIOLENCE

There is a serious concern about the escalation of juvenile violence in this nation. During the 1960s and 1970s, the criminal activity of youth in America was primarily property-related: stealing cars, other theft, and arson. However, the 1980s and 1990s have seen dramatic increases in the number of juveniles involved in crimes related to violence. Many of them are urban, poor, and African American.

The 1990 violent crime arrest rate was 1,429 per 100,000 African American juveniles, five times the rate for white youth (U.S. Department of Justice 1991). The juvenile murder arrest rate for African Americans swelled 145 percent during the 1980s, compared to 48 percent for whites. In 1990 the murder arrest rate for African American juveniles was 7.5 times that of whites. Overall, in the twenty-five years from 1965 to 1990, the murder arrest rate for juveniles rose 332 percent. In addition, the number of juveniles who commit murder with guns had increased 79 percent (ibid.).

Between 1965 and 1990, the overall juvenile forcible rape arrest rate doubled, from 10.9 percent to 21.9 percent. During that period, white arrests increased at a significantly higher rate than did African American arrests, 86 percent versus 9 percent. However, in 1990 the African American arrest rate for forcible rape was about three times that of whites. The percent distribution for forcible rape arrestees in 1990 was 46 percent for African Americans, 53 percent for whites, and 2 percent for others (ibid.).

The arrest rate for juvenile robbery peaked in 1978, declined in the middle 1980s, and began an upward trend in 1988. In 1990 the African American robbery arrest rate was 34 percent higher than in 1988, and the white robbery arrest rate had increased 54 percent since 1988. African Americans constituted 63 percent of juvenile robbery arrests, the highest African American percentage for any violent crime category. The rate of juvenile arrests for aggravated assault has also increased dramatically for both African American and white youth: the arrest rate for African Americans rose 89 percent from 1980 to 1990, compared to 59 percent for whites (ibid.).

Heroin/cocaine violations now represent the predominant drug arrest category for all juveniles, a fact that indicates a relationship between juvenile violence and the growing drug traffic. Between 1980 and 1990, the overall rate of juvenile heroin/cocaine arrests increased an astonishing 713 percent, and the African American arrest rate jumped an even more astonishing 2,373 percent, compared to a 251 percent increase for whites and 127 percent for other groups. The overall arrest rate for marijuana decreased by 66 percent, and the decline was experienced by all racial groups (ibid.).

In the category of weapon law violations, there were 151 arrests per 100,000 juveniles, the highest rate ever recorded. Arrest rate increases between 1980 and 1990 were experienced by both African American and white juveniles, 103 percent and 58 percent respectively, while the "other-race" category experienced a decrease of 48 percent. The percent distribution by race for juvenile weapon law violations arrests in 1990 was 36 percent for African Americans, 62 percent for whites, and 2 percent for other races.

Additional information on African American juvenile arrestees/detainees is provided in the Drug Use Forecasting (DUF) report for 1990 (U.S. Department of Justice 1990). Eleven DUF sites collected interview data from a sample of 225 male juvenile/detainees between the ages of nine and eighteen. African American male juveniles comprised the majority of the sample in six of the eleven DUF sites. The charges on which the juveniles had been arrested and detained included assault, burglary, destruction of property, drug sales/possession, homicide/manslaughter, larceny/theft, probation/parole violation, public peace disturbance, robbery, sex offense, status offense, stolen property/vehicle, weapons, and others. The highest rates for drug sales/possession were 38 percent of the juvenile arrestees in Washington, D.C., 21 percent in Cleveland, 11 percent in St. Louis, 9 percent in Birmingham, and 8 percent in San Diego.

CASE STUDY
Monster Kody

In 1992 South Central Los Angeles, the battlefield of the Crips and the Bloods, erupted. The decay and depression of nearly twenty years exploded as gang members pulled people from their cars, stores, and houses and beat and robbed them. Troops moved in, and Los Angeles was set afire. One of the gang members, Sanyika Shakur, a.k.a. Monster Kody Scott, had lived in South Central Los Angeles all of his life and was recruited into the Crips at the age of eleven. To him,

> *Bangin' ain't no part-time thang, it's full-time, it's a career. It's bein' down when ain't nobody else down with you. It's gettin' caught and not tellin'. Killin' and not caring, and dyin' without fear. It's love for your set and hate for the enemy. (Shakur 1993)*

Kody Scott was initiated into the Crips after he had pumped eight blasts from a sawed-off shotgun into a group of enemy gang members. From that moment, Kody began focusing all of his energy, ambition, and brutality into gang missions and soon became known as "Monster" for his acts of extreme violence. Kody let it be known that gang members are responsible for bringing guns into the gang. Very often, they break into homes and steal guns, and with the influx of drugs and global connections, guns are often brought into gangs by the crate or the truckload. Monster Kody tells how the trials of "standing firm" with the gang include a series of tests in various places—the streets, the Hall (Juvenile Hall, for short-term sentences), Camp (for longer sentences), Youth Authority (for minors, those under age 18), and prison. Each level brings longer and harder time and more prestige for the gang member.

In 1980, when he was sixteen and after committing numerous acts of violence, Monster Kody was arrested for murder. At this time he felt that his life had been totally consumed by all aspects of gang life (ibid.). His bedroom had become a command post, and attacks on other gang members (factions of the Crips set) had frequently been launched from his house. His mother was usually working; his father was out of the picture. Kody and his mom had a strained relationship that consisted of staring contests. Kody said that his clothes, his walk, his talk, and his attitude all reflected his allegiance to his set. Nobody was more important to Kody than his homeboys—not even his family. Kody says that his transformation into the gang lifestyle was subtle and that these kinds of changes are difficult to detect, stop, or prevent.

Monster Kody was acquitted on the murder charge but a year later was charged with robbery and sentenced to four years at Youth Authority. After serving one year, he was back on the street, involved in shoot-outs and gang violence. Eventually he was charged with mayhem and two counts of attempted murder and was taken to county jail. After a fight in prison, he was charged with conspiracy, assault, and arson and wound up in maximum security. Kody went to Soledad Prison to serve a seven-year sentence in 1984 (Bing 1991). While there, he had a confrontation with a guard, stabbed him, and received twenty-eight months in solitary confinement at San Quentin. He was transferred to Folsom Prison, where he was incarcerated until he gained his parole in 1989. Following his release from prison, he was arrested for possession of an AK-47 with three clips of ammunition and sent back to Soledad. After his release from Soledad, he was captured by the Los Angeles Police Department in 1991 for assault and grand theft auto. He was placed in solitary confinement because of his terrible record. Kody feels that the contributing factors that lead African Americans to gang involvement are many and complex and that no group or person has the answer.

PREVENTION

Louis Gonzales (1993) describes some of the early signs of potential gang involvement: poor academic achievement; low self-esteem; resentment of authority; alienation from school, peers, and family; special nicknames; major behavioral problems at home or school; residence in a gang-active neighborhood; friends and relatives in gangs; dressing in clique or gang attire; drug use; and the use of racial or ethnic slurs.

Prevention measures involve enforcing behavior codes; removing graffiti; providing conflict resolution, peer counseling, student assistance, anger management, tutoring, and positive self-esteem programs; employing gang members as "change agents"; offering parenting classes; opening the lines of communication with law enforcement and through youth intervention programs; and developing neighborhood networks, block watches, and patrols.

Deborah Prothrow-Stith (1991) provides recommendations on how to deal with the deadly consequences of gangs, drugs, and violence by addressing the vital role that families play in teaching children to use force to resolve their conflicts. Parents and guardians generally do not tell children and youth to go out and kill or injure people, but they also may not necessarily teach children how to manage anger and aggression in a nonviolent manner.

> The destructive lessons parents teach when they are physically and psychologically abusive to their children and when they allow their children to be physically and psychologically abusive to others, in conjunction with our society's glorification of violence, the ready availability of guns, and the drug culture are an explosive combination that set our children up to be the perpetrators and the victims of violence. (Ibid.: 145)

At least half of all African American girls and boys spend part of their childhood in single parent families, most often headed by women. In some African American families the biological father is absent or not known and there may be a boyfriend or significant man coming in and out of the child's life. Although African American boys and girls alike need to be close to a loving and caring father, the socialization of boys appears to be in greater jeopardy when fathers are missing. Accepting the nonviolent authority of fathers helps African American boys handle their anger and aggression. Fathers and other caring, nonviolent male mentors can make a tremendous difference in preventing gang involvement, violent behavior, and drug involvement on the part of young males. African American males can provide role models and be "surrogate parents" for children and youth who need to learn to manage anger and aggression and develop empathy for the needs of others. Families, schools, and communities should together teach children and youth how to manage anger and aggression in constructive ways.

CONCLUSION

Researchers, law enforcement officials, policy makers, and the general public are recognizing an ever-closer relationship between gangs, drugs, and violence. Expanding drug traffic provides gangs with the income to assume an opulent lifestyle and to acquire the weapons they feel they need to protect their turf and drug operations from one another. In urban neighborhoods held hostage by gang violence, innocent residents live in constant fear for their lives. Gangs are spreading from their original local neighborhoods to urban and rural areas across the nation and can develop and create an environment where the basic social institutions of the family, churches, schools, and community agencies are paralyzed. The value of property decreases, businesses move out, and taxpayers have to pay for increased protection and damage to property in many urban neighborhoods where gangs have established themselves. Gang members have recruited local residents, many of them juveniles, to act as lookouts and drug runners, so that a major concern for families and communities is the increased recruitment of younger children into illegal street activities. Older gang members recruit younger children to sell or run drugs because they insulate the older, adult gang members from arrest. If the gang problem for African American youth is going to be seriously addressed, then families and communities must step up their prevention efforts to keep juveniles from joining gangs. Drug education programs are also critical in the fight against gangs because young people need skills to resist the combined threat of drugs and gangs.

8 THE CHURCH AND ADDICTION

Amazing grace! How sweet the sound
That saved a wretch like me!
I once was lost, but now am found,
Was blind, but now I see.

—John Newton, 1779

John Newton was an English slave trader who repented of his way of life while in a storm at sea. During the storm he wrote "Amazing Grace," a hymn that has inspired African Americans to seek spiritual grace and guidance during the trials and tribulations of life. Today, nearly three out of four African Americans are affiliated with a church community (Lincoln 1989). In order to address drug addiction and African Americans, we have to consider the role of the church as a shaper of African American spiritual beliefs, values, norms, expectations, and behaviors.

THE AFRICAN AMERICAN CHURCH FELLOWSHIP

The African American church, the first fellowship organization to help African Americans deal with the oppression of slavery and a racist society, has been a significant force in the movement of African Americans toward freedom of mind, body, and spirit. There is some difference of opinion among African American church historians regarding the date the first independent church was established. According to Benjamin Mays and Joseph Nicholson (1969 [1933]), this event occurred in Silver Bluff, South Carolina, between 1773 and 1775. Others argue that the oldest African American Baptist church could be the First Colored Baptist Church, started in Savannah, Georgia, in 1779. Early Baptist churches were under white leadership, under African American leadership, or under mixed, shared leadership (Fitts 1985).

In 1787 the Free African Society formed in Philadelphia to confront the segregation and discrimination in the white churches. It provided spiritual support, aid, and fellowship for its members, and two local churches emerged from the society: the African Protestant Episcopal Church of St. Thomas and Bethel African Methodist Episcopal Church opened in July 1794 in Philadelphia. Bethel ended all ties with the white Methodists and became the mother church of the first African American religious denomination, whereas St. Thomas remained a part of the existing white Anglican church community.

THE SEVEN NATIONAL COMMUNIONS

The seven national communions (three Methodist, three Baptist, and one Pentecostal—The Church of God in Christ) include about 84 percent of the African American Christians in the nation (Lincoln 1989). About 16 percent of African American Christians are members of white Protestant and Catholic communions or of a number of small, independent African American churches with limited local or national representation. Islamic communions are not included in Lincoln's breakdown of African American churches, but they represent a growing presence in this nation and must be included in any discussion of faith communities that affect the African American community. The number of African Americans of Muslim faith is difficult to determine accurately, but estimates range from about one hundred thousand to two million.

The majority of African Americans are affiliated with the Baptist denomination. Twelve million African Americans are members of the National Baptist Convention, USA/Inc., the National Baptist Convention of America, and the Progressive National Baptist Convention, Inc. The second largest African American denomination is the Methodist faith, with a combined membership of about six million African Americans.

AFRICAN AMERICAN METHODISTS

Significant numbers of African Americans identified with and joined the Methodist Church at its inception in 1768 because it took a strong antislavery stance. Another attraction of the Methodist Church was its acceptance of African American preachers such as Richard Allen and "Black Harry" Hosier, who traveled with Francis Asbury, the first bishop of the church in America, and who preached to large mixed-race crowds in numerous towns and cities. Some white Methodists who harbored racist beliefs had difficulty accepting the increasing number of African American church members. Physical segregation, denial of common participation in some church rituals, and other forms of discrimination led to the eventual establishment of independent African American Methodist churches. A new denomination called the African-Methodist Episcopal Church (AME) was formed, and Richard Allen, pastor of the African American mother church, Bethel African Episcopal Methodist Church, was elected bishop. The Negro Convention Movement, begun in 1830, assembled African American Christians of all denominations who shared a belief in freedom and the ending of slavery. This was the first political movement of the African American church. In 1856, the AME Church founded Wilberforce University in Ohio, the first Historically Black College. Other AME schools are Morris Brown in Georgia, Paul Quinn in Texas, Richard Allen in South Carolina, and Edward Waters in Florida. In addition to these five colleges, the AME Church provided support for a junior college, two seminaries, and two employment training centers.

A second African American Methodist organization developed early on. In 1793 the membership of the John Street Methodist Church in New York City was about 40 percent African American, and white efforts to keep the church segregated led to a racial crisis within the congregation. In the Methodist churches generally, African Americans sat in separate areas and were refused common celebration of the Eucharist with white members. They also were denied ordination as preachers and membership in the annual convention, which decided matters of church governance. Under the leadership of Peter Williams, a caucus of African Americans formed an African Chapel in 1796. A new church house was built in 1801, and the new church was incorporated as the Zion Church (Lincoln 1989). Eventually, other churches were founded and together formed the African Methodist Episcopal Zion Church, which was invited to merge with the original AME Church but declined in order to maintain its own identity. These so-called Zionites, like the Allenites, were opposed to slavery and became involved in the Underground Railroad, which was known as the Freedom Church. Early members included Harriet Tubman, Frederick Douglass, and Sojourner Truth.

After the Civil War the Christian Methodist Episcopal Church (CME) emerged in a southern branch of the Methodist Episcopal Church that had broken off from the national body over the issue of slavery in 1844. In 1870 representatives of African American churches met and founded a communion that was named the Colored Methodist Episcopal Church in America. This name was modified to Christian Methodist Church in 1954. The church supports five colleges—Lane College in Jackson, Tennessee, Texas College in Tyler, Texas, Paine College in Augusta, Georgia, Miles College in Birmingham, Alabama, and Mississippi Industrial Institute—and Phillips School of Theology. In the late 1800s, African Americans founded a number of small independent African American Methodist communions that included the Reformed Methodist Union Episcopal Church, the African Union First Colored Methodist Protestant Church, the Union American Methodist Episcopal Church, and the Free Christian Zion Church of Christ.

In the early 1900s African Americans continued to struggle against oppression. During this time they founded the National Association for the Advancement of Colored People, the National Urban League, the Negro Independent Movement, the Equal Rights League, and the National Negro Business League. By the mid-1900s, African Americans had achieved recognition in religion, the arts, science, education, business, and industry, despite the historical realities of enormous challenges. The generation of African Americans who lived during the first half of the twentieth century experienced severe discrimination and injustice, and they maintained churches and other institutions under conditions of extreme racism.

One of the most distinguished African American church leaders, Dr. Martin Luther King, Jr., epitomized the struggle against racism and discrimination during the 1950s and 1960s. King's movement had the moral authority of the Christian church and the support of labor leaders and the international community. The civil rights movement he and his Southern Christian Leadership Conference led took much of the focus away from the growing problem of African American drug addiction. While African Americans fought for their civil rights, the use of psychedelic drugs, marijuana, heroin, alcohol, and other drugs was on the rise, especially in the cities.

A MODEL PROGRAM FOR DRUG ABUSE: GLIDE MEMORIAL UNITED METHODIST CHURCH

In the 1960s San Francisco was one of the urban areas where drug use, crime, and the incidence of family disarray were increasing. By the late

1980s, crack cocaine use had reached epidemic proportions in the streets of San Francisco as in many parts of this nation. Reverend Cecil Williams, Minister of Liberation at Glide Memorial United Methodist Church in San Francisco, became extremely concerned about the effect of the drug epidemic on the nation and the local community. In 1989 Glide organized a national conference, "Death of a Race," that drew 1,100 people concerned about the problems of African American addiction to San Francisco.

Glide developed an Afrocentric drug prevention and intervention program based on eleven steps (Williams 1992). These Terms of Faith and Resistance are:

1. Gain control over my life.

2. Tell my story to the world.

3. Stop lying.

4. Be honest with myself.

5. Accept who I am.

6. Feel my real feelings.

7. Feel my pain.

8. Forgive myself and forgive others.

9. Practice rebirth: A new life.

10. Live my spirituality.

11. Support and love my brothers and sisters.

The Substance Abuse Prevention and Recovery Program at Glide Memorial United Methodist Church is a seventeen-week outpatient program that provides unlimited aftercare. Recovery groups (both mixed and separate groups for men and women) meet six days a week, and program staff members are available every day. The program is spiritually based, with an emphasis on empowerment through self-definition. A special program, Women on the Move, provides self-esteem and co-dependency classes and a parent/child reunification program.

Glide also organized It's Recovery Time, marches into housing projects and African American communities. These efforts were not intended to run out the users and the pushers but to bring them into a fellowship of love, hope, acceptance, and recovery from drug abuse. Community-based programs against substance abuse that Glide has initiated incorporate public agencies, the police, tenant associations, and health and social service programs. Through major conferences, the church has created a national network designed to spread a consistent community strategy to assist African Americans in recovery from drugs and violence.

The majority of the addicts who go to Glide for recovery are African Americans, and the central message of the program is that recovery is a miracle of healing and a social change movement. Reverend Williams and the Glide community believed that while the traditional twelve-step programs based on Alcoholics Anonymous provided valuable individual support for recovery, African Americans needed a communal program that incorporated the extended African American family and community. Recovery at Glide includes recognition of the power of addiction, development of a sense of personal self-definition, a feeling of rebirth that comes from facing the pain and telling the truth, and a sense of community that includes redefining relationships with African Africans and people of all races, cultures, and classes.

AFRICAN AMERICAN BAPTISTS

The early African American Baptist churches were founded in the southeastern slave states before the Civil War. In these early churches, African American Christians struggled to provide spiritual support for each other during slavery. Because of the strict controls of slavery, however, few such churches emerged until after the Civil War. Prior to the war, in many churches in the South, African American members had outnumbered white, but whites controlled the church and subjected the African American members to humiliation, rejection, discrimination, and prejudice. When they could, African American Baptists formed their own churches—in Virginia, Georgia, Boston, New York, and Philadelphia. After numerous attempts to bring these widely scattered churches into one organizational framework, the National Baptist Convention, USA/Inc. (NBCI) was formed in 1895, and it remains the largest African American Protestant organization in the world. It has been reported that NBCI has a membership of 7.1 million people, about one-fourth of the estimated African American population of the United States. The African American Baptist churches support many well-known colleges, including Morehouse, Benedict, Spelman, Shaw, Virginia Union, Turner Theological Seminary in Atlanta, and the American Baptist Theological Seminary in Nashville.

The National Baptist Convention of America (NBCA) developed out of a publishing house dispute that occurred in 1915 with the NBCI. In 1961 the Progressive National Baptist Convention (PNBC) developed from another conflict within the NBCI. Long-standing policy disagreements resulted in a rupture that was led by Dr. Gardner Taylor, Dr. Benjamin Mays, Martin Luther King, Sr., Martin Luther King, Jr., Ralph Abernathy, and others who were opposed to conservative policies that they felt stood in the way of the civil rights movement in America. The PNBC was deeply involved in the civil rights movement, opposed the Vietnam War, stresses political and economic development, and includes more liberal pastors in its membership.

A MODEL PROGRAM FOR DRUG ABUSE:
MT. ZION BAPTIST CHURCH

In Seattle, Washington, a number of community leaders began holding discussions about the horrors of crack cocaine, with the assistance of the Reverend Samuel Berry McKinney, senior pastor at Mt. Zion Baptist Church, the largest African American church in the Pacific Northwest. Under the leadership of the Reverend Stephen Lloyd Johnson, an associate pastor at Mt. Zion, a new organization called the Cocaine Outreach and Recovery Program (CORP) was formed in 1989. CORP is sponsored by the church and has developed an Afrocentric approach to recovery from drug abuse.

In 1991 CORP sponsored a national conference, "Confronting Addiction in the African American Family and Community: Working for Hope, Healing, and Recovery," that drew an audience of seven hundred people concerned about the epidemic of addiction. This was the first such conference to be held in the Pacific Northwest and was inspired by the efforts, faith, and commitment of the Reverend Cecil Williams of Glide Memorial United Methodist Church. CORP organized and hosted this conference because its members believed that the crack epidemic could be stopped only if all members of the community work together for the healing of neighborhoods and cities.

Programs emerged from this conference that addressed the needs of African Americans addicted to drugs. In 1991 CORP produced an acclaimed booklet, *Getting Off Crack*, which has been widely distributed throughout the nation. This booklet provides essential information on asking for help, finding an appropriate recovery program, breaking away from old friends and old playgrounds, dealing with money, being honest, finding a higher power, and telling your story.

CORP has developed family recovery retreats on a small island in the Puget Sound. These retreats focus on talking about feelings, patterns of addiction, hope, healing, and recovery for African Americans. The program also sponsors separate groups for men, for women, and for families that focus on sharing feelings and drug abuse issues.

In order to determine how well programs like CORP are working, one needs to define success and take a baseline measure of the individual's situation when he or she is starting on the road to recovery. The main problems encountered for those needing services include limited resources such as insurance, housing, food, and friends; a well-developed pattern of deception and denial of drug use; a limited experience in completing tasks or achieving goals; and a history of traumatic events that have not been healed. Given this array of problems, success for the program should be defined on a case-by-case basis in terms of how well the individual abstained from drugs and became a functional member of society. The CORP model endorses the disease model of addiction (a physiological disease that is primary, progressive, and fatal) and attempts to find the root cause of the addiction and to get the disease into remission. The Glide model, as an Afrocentric model, attempts to reconnect the individual to his or her culture and self-pride, changes essential to recovery.

AFRICAN AMERICAN PENTECOSTALS

After the Civil War independent urban African American churches became well established and successful. Many of these churches, however, had lost their enthusiasm for the fight against prejudice, discrimination, and injustice, leading to the emergence of two African American church movements: the Sanctified and Holiness movements. The Sanctified movement was a response to conflict over changes in worship traditions (Gilkes 1985). Sanctified Church members felt certain trends devalued African Americans, such as white people addressing African American women and men by their first names and white church members not being supportive of social, economic, and political change. The

Holiness movement grew out of the Methodist doctrine and was later to become the foundation of the Pentecostal movement (MacRobert 1988).

The Pentecostal movement developed under the leadership of William Seymour, an African American Holiness radical preacher who led the Azusa Street Revival in Los Angeles from 1906. Seymour added "speaking in tongues," as occurred at the Feast of Pentecost following the resurrection of Jesus, to the traditional Holiness doctrines of salvation and sanctification. The Pentecostal faith was originally interracial, but it split into different denominations, including the African American Church of God in Christ and the white Assemblies of God. Some Holiness churches added Pentecostal to their names; others resisted such identification; and in some other cases, elements of Pentecostalism known as "the charismatic movement" became a part of churches in other denominations. Pentecostalism is the only African American Christian communion without white origins. Ironically, William Seymour in Los Angeles and Charles Harrison Mason in Mississippi ordained white preachers by the hundreds who then founded their own churches or denominations, such as the Pentecostal Fellowship of North America and the National Association of Evangelicals, which did not allow African Americans to become members.

AFRICAN AMERICANS IN
THE CHURCH OF GOD IN CHRIST

In 1897 the Church of God in Christ (COGIC) was organized in Memphis, Tennessee, by Charles Harrison Mason, a former Baptist pastor. Mason was dismissed from his Baptist church because of his experience of "sanctification" in 1893. At an Azusa Street Revival in Los Angeles, Mason experienced the "gift of tongues," and his church made the transition from Holiness to Pentecostal. COGIC is a rapidly growing African American denomination, second only to the National Baptist Convention, Inc. COGIC supports several hundred churches, schools, clinics, and orphanages in Africa, India, Sri Lanka, Haiti, and other developing nations and sponsors bible colleges, a junior college, and a seminary in Atlanta.

Smaller African American Pentecostal denominations are the United Holy Church of America, the United House of Prayer for All People, the Fire Baptized Holiness Church of God of the Americas, and the Sought Out Church of God in Africa Universal Church.

THE URBAN AFRICAN AMERICAN CHURCH

The Great Migration of African Americans from the South to the North placed many African Americans in unfamiliar settings. According to Ida Rousseau Mukenge (1983), the African American church of this time period faced the internal problems of power and wealth and external problems created by competing organizations. As the northern African American population increased over time, its needs and wants became very diverse. Churches were property holders and were often faced with significant financial obligations. As a result church leaders focused their energy on maintaining or developing large memberships to meet mortgages and ministers' salaries. Many African Americans were dismayed by these larger, more formal churches as they searched for worship services with a familiar southern flavor. The urban churches did not make the migrants feel welcome and continued to be monopolized by the older members (Baer 1984; Frazier 1934; Wilmore 1972).

The African American church in the early 1900s shifted its focus away from racial matters and its efforts to reach African Americans from a wide variety of social and economic backgrounds (Mukenge 1983). It gradually became a church focused on social class lines within the congregation. As a result, the church did not address the spiritual or social needs of many migrants. These conditions were fertile ground for the development of movements like Holiness, Pentecostalism, and Spiritualist in the early 1900s and the Nation of Islam in the 1930s, movements that focused on meeting spiritual and material needs, in addition to developing self-pride and self-sufficiency through the promotion of African American–owned banks, restaurants, clothing stores, schools, farms, bakeries, supermarkets, publishing companies, and other businesses.

THE HISTORICAL CHURCH:
SHAPER OF AFRICAN AMERICAN CULTURE

The African American churches, preachers, and congregations have been important shapers of African American spiritual, cultural, social, economic, educational, and political life in the United States from the time of slavery to the present. The church has been a dominant force and a symbol of hope and spiritual presence for the African American family. It has provided support for fighting for freedom from slavery and oppression, instilling pride, developing ambition, creating music, promoting education, training orators, exerting political power, and developing racial and ethnic identity. The African American church has also been a catalyst for the establishment of fraternities, sororities, banks, insurance companies, educational programs and institutions, and social programs.

The historical African American church provided a buffer against the dehumanizing effects of racial segregation, discrimination, and bigotry and has provided a safe place for the emotional release of concerns and feelings that could not have been safely expressed in white churches or white society. The church has thrived because of the strong belief African American Christians hold that the burdens of life would eventually be lifted in the promised land. Some researchers argue that slaves identified themselves with the oppressed Israelites, felt that the slaveholders were like the cruel Egyptians, and believed that Canaan was the land of freedom (Calverton 1940).

While the historical church provided cohesion and support within the African American community, church ministers and leaders were essentially not in favor of directly reacting to the racial situation in America. Prior to the civil rights movement the approach to institutional and individual racism was a conservative and gradual effort to change social and economic inequalities. In the early days of the African American church, it stressed family, social, and economic concerns. The church offered a sense of community, personal and psychological support, coping strategies, role models, and a sense of collective achievement and emphasized active involvement in church fellowship, organizations, and networks.

THE AFRICAN AMERICAN CHURCH TODAY

The African American church today is the result of a historical evolution. It developed in response to the needs and demands of African Americans who retained a belief in the harmony of spiritual and physical life (Washington and Beasley 1988) and today is clearly represented by a variety of denominations that have been both proactive and reactive in providing assistance, encouraging empowerment, and fighting for social change. The African American church continues to function as an institution that affects the psychological and social health of African Americans for the good of the community.

CONCLUSION

Religion, the African American church, and behavioral change need to be examined further to better understand the difficulties the church faces in addressing drug addiction. Religion is a set of beliefs, rituals, ceremonies, symbols, sacred references, and culturally patterned interactions (Crippen 1988; Hammond 1988; Spiro 1966) that represent the thinking of groups such as Baptists, Methodists, Pentecostals, and Muslims. The African American church, a social organization based on religious tenets, is both a psychological bridge and a physical building that allows individuals an opportunity to connect with a group in order to experience a sense of togetherness and mutual support.

Murray Levine (1988), in a review of mutual support groups, outlined key features of mutual assistance, such as developing an ideology that stresses belonging, promoting a sense of community, providing role models, teaching effective coping strategies for day-to-day problems, and providing a network of social relationships. These are features that have been exhibited by the African American church throughout its history. Thus, opportunities have been made available through the African American church that were not available in the larger society.

It is extremely difficult for the African American church to develop programs to treat drug addiction because the focus of these programs is based on the need for behavioral change. Psychology, the discipline with important knowledge in the area of human behavior, however, is based on very different assumptions than those of the church. The foundation of religious beliefs is faith, whereas psychology focuses on the workings of the mind and behaviors. The African American church has focused primarily on nurturing the spiritual needs of individuals or groups, which in turn can affect the social life of individuals. Some African American church leaders view the church's primary function as a religious worship center and have no desire to develop social service programs. For these church leaders, there is a very strong belief that good preaching—connecting the word with the spirit—provides the inner strength that people need in order to deal with social problems. While nurturing the spiritual needs of addicts is important and necessary, it is not enough for the drug addict who needs to change attitudes and behaviors.

The church needs to be restructured to move beyond the one-dimensional perspective of providing spiritual refuge and regular worship to the multidimensional perspective of providing for the full needs of its members and the greater community. The African American church of the 1990s is beginning to face the challenges of drug abuse, child care, food and housing, individual and family counseling, job opportunities, teenage mothers and fathers, racism, education, and health care. More traditional concerns such as good preaching, regular revivals, and social fellowship are giving way to addressing the social needs of the African American community. However, often only the larger urban churches are endowed with the financial resources and trained staff needed to address contemporary social problems and challenges.

CONCLUSION

Examining the historic and current alcohol and other drug use patterns of African Americans has been a fascinating and a frightening task. We have attempted to look at African American addiction objectively, yet our examination of increasing levels of alcoholism and addiction in our communities has brought us face-to-face with serious patterns of addiction that have alarmed and shaken us.

Our research was designed to determine the most common and frequent patterns of addiction in African American communities. This book began with an overview of these patterns, but we were compelled to examine areas that we felt demanded closer attention. Our examination of African American alcohol and other drug use prior to and during slavery convinced us that additional research is needed in this area. Do patterns of family alcoholism that started over one hundred years ago during slavery somehow play a generative role in the current epidemic of addiction? Do family patterns of alcoholism relate to current patterns of crack cocaine addiction? How different from urban patterns are the patterns of alcohol and other drug use by rural African American populations? These are but a few of the areas that deserve additional research and investigation.

It is important for future research to investigate how addiction and racism interact. Continued research into the economic consequences of racism that encourage the development of addiction in African American communities needs attention, and the use of alcohol and other drugs to relieve the emotional pain of racism in African American people should also receive further study. Indeed, African American success in recovery from drug use may depend in part on the strength of the link between racism and addiction.

Our study and reflection have convinced us that several distinct patterns of addiction exist in African American communities. The first pattern is a period of intense work followed by short-term weekend drug use. This pattern of drug use began during slavery as slavemasters worked slaves without relief, especially in crop planting, maintenance, and harvesting. The slaves were then given alcohol after harvesting and during special events and holidays, as a reward for working hard. Thus, various alcoholic beverages, including rum and whiskey, became material rewards that slaves received for their labor, and alcohol use became a conditioned response and a reward system following hard work. Prior to this time, the cultural experience of the slaves had been limited to relatively mild intoxicants such as beer and palm wine used for social and sacred use in African tribal society.

A second pattern is that of African Americans engaging in alcohol- and drug-related income-producing activities. During oppressive colonial and post–Civil War economies, the survival of African Americans often became dependent on the organization of illegal alternative economies that supported the vices of the white population. After the end of slavery, some enterprising African Americans in the South developed illegal saloons, alcohol distilleries, houses of prostitution, gambling joints, and other illegal businesses that served white customers, as there were limited mainstream education and employment opportunities for African Americans. Those who migrated to the North found less rigid forms of segregation and they too were able to set up illegal drug-related businesses that served whites, businesses that provided a dependable source of income. Over time, African Americans in large numbers became customers of illegal drug-related businesses. Currently, a significant percentage of the urban African American population continues to earn income from drug sales, preparation, and marketing. In many urban communities, African Americans are disproportionately represented in the population of males incarcerated for drug sales.

A third pattern that stands out is the differences in general between the criminal penalties received by African American citizens for drug-related offenses and the penalties others receive. Since the early 1900s drug possession and drug dealing have consistently resulted in longer sentences for African American offenders and also in different kinds of penalties. From the 1930s to the 1960s African American addicts were placed in federal treatment hospitals or incarcerated in federal prisons, whereas most of the country's majority-culture addicts went through private hospital systems or to state mental hospitals. This pattern of African American addicts ending up in jail while white addicts are placed on probation and in treatment has been repeated in the crack cocaine epidemic. The penalties for the possession or sale of drugs predominately used in the white community—methamphetamine (speed) and powder cocaine—are probation, treatment, or imprisonment; white offenders receive jail time only about half as often as do African Americans who use crack cocaine.

The impact of such sentencing practices on the African American community has been horrendous in the past ten years. Individuals with the disease of addiction are removed from their homes and communities and lose their employment. Children lose parents, families lose income-producing members, and extended family relationships break up. Individuals come back to their families, not cured, but further traumatized by their imprisonment. Their addictions remain virtually untreated and have often gotten worse in prison. The trauma and loss of dignity such imprisonment causes communities, families, and individuals is a key factor in the growth of gangs, teen violence, and child abuse. The most vulnerable children are left without parents and protectors in a violent and insane drug culture.

A fourth pattern is the tolerance of the epidemic of addiction in African American communities by public health officials and community leaders. Few solutions to epidemic addiction in African American communities are being offered by public health officials and community leaders. The high levels of alcoholism in older African American males and increasing levels of addiction to crack cocaine in younger African Americans have elicited little public response. African American urban communities are in their second decade of a crack cocaine epidemic and yet there is no national plan from African American leaders and public health officials to treat the ongoing loss of lives. The proliferation of crack houses and the easy distribution of crack cocaine in the African American community endangers the stability of major cities.

A VISION OF AFRICAN AMERICAN RECOVERY

Real solutions to the continuing threat of addiction in African American communities must involve community, state, and federal policy. It is our belief that African American church, community, and media leadership can make a significant difference in recovery rates and the prevention of addiction in urban areas. Partnerships between federal, state, and local agencies and African American churches can be effective in reducing and eliminating patterns of addiction. The African American church is located in the community where drug addiction is widespread, and the church represents the greatest economic, spiritual, and social resource within the community. African American churches should receive support, training, and funds for drug prevention. The African American church should be the wall of defense against drug use, and the community should make the children of addicts and alcoholics a primary prevention population.

Another solution to epidemic addiction in the African American community is the development and expansion of existing programs that are culturally relevant to the African American experience. Many prevention and treatment programs are designed for the majority community and are viewed as transportable to the African American community. Programs for African Americans have to be designed to focus on specific populations such as addicted women who have been sexually abused, older male alcoholics, and gang members who use drugs to deal with loss of family and relationships. The treatment programs that address the various learning styles of these special populations will lead to a greater understanding of their unique recovery needs.

Another vision for African American recovery from addiction stresses the elimination of alcohol and cigarette advertising in African American media. Numerous national magazines and community newspapers are highly dependent on the advertising of alcohol and cigarette companies. Sponsorship of community events by such companies promotes a positive image of these products and underplays the lethal impact they have on the health of African Americans.

Many lessons are to be learned from the history of the patterns of addiction in the African American community. This book should serve as a powerful reminder of the need to develop culturally competent and appropriate prevention, intervention, treatment, and aftercare programs for African Americans in order to address patterns of addiction. An understanding of the historical, social, political, psychological, cultural, economic, and environmental dimensions of these patterns is a fundamental tool we must provide to those who face the critical challenge of stopping the epidemic of addiction.

BIBLIOGRAPHY

Aaron, P., and D. Musto. 1979. Temperance in America: A historical overview. Unpublished draft prepared for the Panel on Alternative Policies Affecting the Prevention of Alcohol Abuse and Alcoholism of the National Research Council. December.

Alcoholics Anonymous. 1976. *The Big Book*. New York: Alcoholics Anonymous World Services, Inc.

Alcohol Information Research Services. 1987. Liquor industry wants larger share of black market. *Bottom Line* 8, 2:13–14.

Allen, N. 1978. *The Opium Trade*. Boston: Longwood Press.

American Medical Association, Council on Mental Health. 1957. *Report on Narcotic Addiction*.

Anderson, J. 1981. New York Harlem. Part 3. *The New Yorker*, July 13, 38–79.

Anslinger, H. J., and W. F. Tompkins. 1953. *The Traffic in Narcotics*. New York: Funk and Wagnalls.

Asbury, H. 1950. *The Great Illusion*. New York: Doubleday.

Ashley, R. Cocaine. 1975. *Its History, Uses and Effects*. New York: St. Martin's Press.

Bachman, J., J. Wallace, P. O'Malley, L. Johnston, C. Kurth, and H. Neighbors. 1991. Racial/ethnic differences in smoking, drinking, and illicit drug use among American high school seniors, 1976–89. *American Journal of Public Health* 81, 3:372–377.

Baer, H. A. 1984. *The Black Spiritual Movement*. Knoxville: The University of Tennessee Press.

Ball, J. C., and C. D. Chambers. 1970. *The Epidemiology of Opiate Addiction in the United States.* Springfield, Ill.: Charles Thomas.

Barnes, G., and J. Welte. 1986a. Adolescent alcohol abuse: Subgroup differences and relationships to other social problem behaviors. *Journal of Adolescent Research* 1, 1:79–94.

———. 1986b. Patterns and predictors of alcohol use among 7–12 grade students in New York State. *Journal of Studies on Alcohol* 47, 1:53–62.

Bates, W. M. 1968. Occupational characteristics of Negro addicts. *International Journal of the Addictions* 3:345–350.

Beck, K., and M. Zannis. 1992. Patterns of alcohol consumption among suburban adolescent black high school students. *Journal of Alcohol and Drug Education* 37, 2:1–13.

Behrens, U. J., T. M. Worner, L. F. Braly, F. Schaffner, and C. S. Lieber. 1988. Carbohydrate deficient transferring, a marker for chronic alcohol consumption in different ethnic populations. *Alcoholism* 12:427–432.

Beidelman, T. O. 1961. Beer drinking and cattle theft in Tanganyika. *American Anthropologist* 63:534–549.

Bell, Peter. 1990. *Chemical Dependency and the African American: Counseling Strategies and Community Issues.* Center City, Minn.: Hazelden Publications.

Bell, Peter, and J. Evans. 1981. *Counseling the Black Client: Alcohol Use and Abuse in Black America.* Hazelden Foundation.

Bing, L. 1991. *Do or Die.* New York: HarperCollins.

Bourne, P. G. 1973. Alcoholism in the urban Negro population. In P. G. Bourne and R. Fox, eds., *Alcoholism progress in research and treatment.* New York: Academic Press.

Brecher, E. M. 1972. Licit and illicit drugs. In *The Consumers Union Report.* Boston: Little Brown.

Breo, D. L. 1993. Kicking butts—AMA, Joe Camel, and the "Black Flag" war on tobacco. *Journal of the American Medical Association,* October 27.

Brisbane, F. L., and M. Womble. 1985. *Treatment of Black Alcoholics.* New York: Haworth Press, Inc.

Brook, J., A. Gordon, A. Brook, and D. Brook. 1989. The consequences of marijuana use on intrapersonal and interpersonal functioning in black and white adolescents. *Genetic, Social, and General Psychology Monographs* 115: 351–369.

Brook, J., B. Hamburg, E. Balka, and P. Wynn. 1992. Sequence of drug involvement in African American and Puerto Rican adolescents. *Psychological Reports* 71, 1:179–182.

Brown, C. 1965. *Manchild in the promised land.* New York: Signet.

Brown, F., and J. Tooley. 1989. Alcoholism in the black community. In G. W. Lawson and A. W. Lawson, eds., *Alcoholism and Substance Abuse in Special Populations.* Rockville, Md.: Aspen Publishers. Pp. 115–130.

Brown, W. K. 1978. Black gangs as family extensions. *International Journal of Offender Therapy and Comparative Criminology* 22, 1:39–45.

Calverton, V. F. 1940. The Negro and American culture. *Saturday Review of Literature,* September 21, 1940, pp. 17f.

Carter, E. 1928. Prohibition and the Negro. *Opportunity* 6, 12:359–360.

Catalano, R., D. Morrison, E. Wells, and M. Gillmore. 1992. Ethnic differences in family factors related to early drug initiation. *Journal of Studies on Alcohol* 53, 3:208–217.

Ceiza de León, P. 1883. *The Second Part of the Chronicles of Peru*. Trans. and edited with notes and an introduction by Clements R. Markham, C.B., F.R.S. London: Hakluyt Society.

Chambers, C. D., and L. Brill. 1973. *Methadone: Experiences and Issues*. New York: Behavioral Publications.

Chambers, C. D., and M. T. Harter. 1987. The epidemiology of narcotics abuse among Blacks in the United States: 1935–1980. In C. D. Chambers et al., eds., *Chemical Dependencies: Patterns, Costs and Consequences*. Athens, Ohio: Ohio University Press. Pp. 191–223.

Chambers, C. D., and A. D. Moffett. 1970. Negro opiate addiction. In J. C. Ball and C. D. Chambers, eds., *The Epidemiology of Opiate Addiction in the United States*. Springfield, Ill.: Charles C. Thomas.

Clark, W. B., and M. E. Hilton. 1991. *Alcohol in America: Drinking Practices and Problems*. Albany: State University of New York Press.

Clausen, J. A. 1961. Drug Addiction. In R. K. Merton and R. A. Nisbet, eds., *Contemporary Social Problems*. New York: Harcourt Brace and World.

Cobb, Thomas R. R. 1858. *An Historical Sketch of Slavery*. Philadelphia: T. and J. W. Johnson & Company.

Coughlin, D. 1992. Smoking guns. *Village Voice*, April 21, 11.

Crippen, T. 1988. Old and new gods in the modern world: Towards a theory of religious transformation. *Social Forces* 7:316–336.

Crogman, W. H. 1903. *Progress of a Race*. Atlanta: J. L. Nichols & Company.

Crother, T. 1902. *Morphism and Narcomanias from Other Drugs: Their Etiology, Treatment and Medicolegal Relations*. Philadelphia: W. B. Saunders.

Dai, B. 1937. *Opium Addiction in Chicago*. Shanghai: Commercial Press.

Davidson, B. 1961. *The African Slave Trade*. Boston: Little, Brown.

———. 1966. *Africa: History of a Continent*. New York: Macmillan.

de Barros, Paul. 1993. *Jackson Street After Hours*. Seattle: Sasquatch Books.

De La Rosa, M. R., E. Lambert, and G. Gropper. 1990. Drugs and violence: Causes, correlates, and consequences. NIDA Research Monograph No. 103. DHHS Pub. No. (ADM)91-1721. Washington, D.C.: GPO.

De La Rosa, M. R., and F. I. Soriano. 1992. Understanding criminal activity and use of alcohol and cocaine derivatives by multi-ethnic gang members. In R. C. Cervantes, ed., *Substance Abuse and Gang Violence*. Newbury Park, Calif.: SAGE Publications. Pp. 24–39.

DeLuca, J., ed. 1981. Fourth Special Report to the U.S. Congress. Washington, D.C.: U.S. Department of Health and Human Services. Alcohol, Drug Abuse and Mental Health Administration, National Institute on Alcohol Abuse and Alcoholism.

Dembo, R., L. Williams, L. La Voie, A. Getreu, E. Berry, L. Genung, J. Schmeidler, E. D. Widh, and J. Kern. 1990. A longitudinal study of the relationship among alcohol use, marijuana/hashish use, cocaine use and cohort of high risk youths. *International Journal of the Addictions* 25:1333–1374.

DeQuincey, T. 1907. *Confessions of an English Opium-Eater*. New York: E. P. Dutton.

Dole, V. P., and M. E. Nyswander. 1967. Heroin addiction: A metabolic disease. *Archives of Internal Medicine* 120, no. 1:19–24.

Douglass, F. 1892. *Life and Times of Frederick Douglass.* Washington, D.C.: Author. Reprinted in 1962 by Macmillan.

Drake, St. C., and H. Cayton. 1945 (1962). *Black Metropolis: A Study of Negro Life in a Northern City.* Vols. 1 and 2. New York and Evanston: Harper and Row.

Dreser, H. 1898. Pharmakologisches ueber einige Morphinderivate. *Therap. Monatschr.* 12:509–512.

Dupont, R. L. 1991. *Crack Cocaine: A Challenge for Prevention.* OSAP Prevention Monograph-9. United States Department of Health and Human Services.

du Toit, B. M. 1991. *Cannabis, Alcohol, and the South African Student: Adolescent Drug Use, 1974–1985.* Athens: Ohio University Center for International Studies Monographs in International Studies. Africa Series No. 59.

Edgerton, Robert. 1988. Foreword. In J. D. Vigil, *Barrio Gangs: Street Life and Identity in Southern California.* Austin: University of Texas Press.

Erikson, E. H. 1982. *The Life Cycle Completed.* New York: Norton.

Essence. 1991. December.

Fitts, L. 1985. *A History of Black Baptists.* Nashville: Broadman Press.

Fox, J. R. 1985. Mission impossible? Social work practice with Black urban youth gangs. *Social Work* 30, 1:25–31.

Franklin, J. H. 1967. *From Slavery to Freedom: A History of Negro Americans.* 3rd ed. New York: Vintage.

Frazier, E. Franklin. 1932. *The Negro Family in Chicago, USA.* Chicago: University of Chicago Press.

———. 1934. Traditions and patterns of Negro family life in the United States. In E. B. Reuter, ed., *Race and Culture Contacts.* New York: McGraw-Hill.

———. 1939. *The Negro Family in the United States.* Chicago: University of Chicago Press.

Genovese, E. D. 1976. *Roll Jordan, Roll: The World the Slaves Made.* New York: Vintage Books.

Gilkes, C. T. 1985. Together and in harness: Women's traditions in the sanctified church signs. *Journal of Women in Culture and Society* 10:678–699.

Glick, R., and J. Moore. 1990. *Drugs in Hispanic Communities.* New Brunswick, N.J.: Rutgers University Press.

Gonzales, L. 1993. Gangs: What parents, schools, and communities need to know. *Adolescence* 5, 6:31–35.

Greene, L. J. 1942. *The Negro in Colonial New England.* New York: Columbia University Press.

Gugliotta, G., and J. Lean. 1989. *Kings of Cocaine.* New York: Harper and Row.

Gurr, T. A. 1989. *Violence in America: Protest, Rebellion, Reform.* Newbury Park, Calif.: SAGE Publications.

Gwinnell, W. B. 1928. Shifting populations in great northern cities. *Opportunity* 6:279.

Hacker, G., R. Collins, and M. Jacobson. 1987. *Marketing Booze to Blacks.* Washington, D.C.: Center for Science in the Public Interest.

Hagedorn, J., with P. Macon. 1988. *People and Folks: Gangs, Crime and the Underclass in a Rustbelt City.* Chicago: Lake View Press.

Hamid, A. 1990. The political economy of crack-related violence. *Journal of Contemporary Drug Problems* 17, 31–78.

Hammond, P. E. 1988. Religion and the persistence of identity. *Journal for the Scientific Study of Religion* 27:1–11.

Harford, T., and C. Lowman. 1982. *Alcohol Use in a National Sample of Black and Non-Black Senior High School Students.* National Institute on Alcohol Abuse and Alcoholism, November 4, 1982.

Harper, F. D. 1976. Etiology: Why do blacks drink? In F. D. Harper, ed., *Alcohol Abuse and Black America.* Alexandria, Va.: Douglass Publishers, Inc.

———. 1988. Alcohol and black youth: An overview. *Journal of Drug Issues* 18, 1:7–14.

———. 1989. Alcoholism and blacks: An overview. In T. D. Watts and R. Wright, eds., *Alcoholism in Minority Populations.* Springfield, Ill.: Charles C. Thomas. Pp. 17–31.

Healy, W. 1915. *The Individual Delinquent.* Boston: Little, Brown.

Heath, D. 1975. A critical review of ethnographic studies of alcohol use. In R. J. Gibbins et al., eds., *Research Advances in Alcohol and Drug Problems.* Vol. 2. New York: John Wiley and Sons.

Helmreich, W. B. 1973. Race, sex, and gangs. *Society* 11: 44–50.

Henningfield, J., R. Clayton, and W. Pollin. 1990. Involvement of tobacco in alcoholism and illicit drug use. *British Journal of Addiction to Alcohol and Other Drugs* 85, 2:279–291.

Hentoff, N. 1968. *A Doctor among the Addicts.* New York: Rand McNally.

Herd, D. 1983. Prohibition, racism and class politics in the post-Reconstruction South. *Journal of Drug Issues* 13, 1:77–94.

———. 1985. Migration, cultural transformation and the rise of black liver cirrhosis mortality. *British Journal of Addiction to Alcohol and Other Drugs* 80: 397–410.

———. 1988a. Black-White differences in drinking problems among U.S. males. Paper presented at the 35th International Congress of the International Council on Alcohol and Addictions, Oslo, Norway, August, 1988.

———. 1988b. Drinking by black and white women: Results from a national survey. *Social Problems* 35, 5:493–520.

———. 1989. The epidemiology of drinking patterns and alcohol-related problems among U.S. Blacks. *NIAAA Research Monograph Series* 18:3–50.

———. 1991. The paradox of temperance: Blacks and the alcohol question in nineteenth-century America. In S. Barrows and R. Room, eds., *Drinking: Behavior and Belief in Modern History.* Berkeley: University of California Press. Pp. 354–375.

———. 1991. We cannot stagger to freedom: A history of blacks and alcohol in American politics. In L. Brill and C. Winick, eds., *Yearbook of Substance Use and Abuse,* vol. 3. New York: Human Sciences Press. Pp. 141–186.

Hoffer, T. A. N., and R. C. Cervantes. 1992. Psychological effects of exposure to gang violence. In R. C. Cervantes, ed., *Substance Abuse and Gang Violence.* Newbury Park, Calif.: SAGE Publications. Pp. 121–135.

Homer. *Odyssey X,* 220–232.

Huff, R. 1990. *Gangs in America.* Newbury Park, Calif.: SAGE Publications.

Inciardi, J. A., D. Lockwood, and A. E. Pottieger. 1993. *Women and Crack Cocaine.* New York: Macmillan.

Irwin, W. 1908. More about 'nigger gin.' *Collier's,* August 15.

Jackson, M. S. 1992. Drug use patterns among black male juvenile delinquents. *Journal of Alcohol and Drug Education* 37, 2:64–70.

Jacobs, H. 1861. *Incidents in the Life of a Slave Girl.* New York: Oxford University Press.

Johnson, D. 1992. Tobacco Stains: Cigarette firms buy into African-American groups. *Progressive* 56, 12:26–28.

Johnson, G. G. 1937. *Ante-bellum North Carolina.* Chapel Hill: University of North Carolina Press.

Johnson, N. C., and S. D. Young. 1992. Survivor's response to gang violence. In R. C. Cervantes, ed., *Substance Abuse and Gang Violence.* Newbury Park, Calif.: SAGE Publications. Pp. 136–146.

Johnson, S. 1989. *Getting Off Crack.* A publication of the Cocaine Outreach and Recovery Program, P.O. Box 3263, Seattle, Washington.

Johnston, L., P. O'Malley, J. Bachman. 1985. *Use of Licit and Illicit Drugs by America's High School Students, 1975–1984.* Rockville, Md.: National Institute on Drug Abuse.

Kandel, D. B. 1975. Reaching the hard-to-reach: Illicit drug use among high school absentees. *Addictive Diseases* 13:465–480.

Kane, H. H. 1882. *Opium-smoking in America and China.* New York: G. P. Putnam's Sons.

Keiser, R. 1969. *The Vice Lord: Warriors of the Streets.* New York: Holt, Rinehart and Winston.

Kennedy, L. W., and W. Baron-Stephen. 1993. Routine activities and a subculture of violence: A study of violence on the street. *Journal of Research in Crime and Delinquency* 30, 1:88–112.

Killion, R. 1973. *Slavery Time.* Savannah: The Beehive Press.

Kim, A., M. Galanter, R. Castaneda, H. Lifshutz, and L. M. King. 1981. Alcoholism: Studies regarding Black Americans: 1977–1980. *Alcohol and Health Monograph No. 4: Special Population Issues.* Washington, D.C.: U.S. GPO. Pp. 385–407.

Kim, A., M. Galanter, R. Castaneda, H. Lifshutz, and H. Franco. 1992. Crack cocaine use and sexual behavior among psychiatric inpatients. *American Journal of Drug and Alcohol Abuse* 18, 3:235–246.

Kleiner, R. J., R. S. Holger, and J. Lanahan. 1975. A study of Black youth groups: Implications for research, action, and the role of the investigator. *Human Organization* 34:391–393.

Kletzing, H. F., and W. H. Crogman. 1903. *Progress of a Race.* Atlanta: J. L. Nichols and Company.

Kotlowitz, A. 1991. *There Are No Children Here: The Story of Two Boys Growing Up in the Other America.* New York: Bantam Doubleday Dell Publishing Group.

Kramer, J. C. 1979. Opium rampant: Medical use, misuse and abuse in Britain and the West in the 17th and 18th centuries. *British Journal of Addiction to Alcohol and Other Drugs* 74, 4:377–389.

Kritikos, P. G., and S. N. Papadaki. 1967. The History of the poppy and of opium and their expansion in antiquity in the eastern Mediterranean area. *Bulletin of Narcotics* 19:17–38.

Kunnes, R. 1972. *The American Heroin Empire: Power, Profits, and Politics*. New York: Dodd, Mead.

Lale, T. S. 1992. Gangs and drugs. In G. W. and A. W. Lawson, eds., *Adolescent Substance Abuse: Etiology, Treatment, and Prevention*. Gaithersburg, Md.: Aspen Publishers. Pp. 267–281.

Larkins, J. 1965. *Alcohol and the Negro: Explosive Issues*. Zebulon, N.C.: Record.

———. 1976. Historical background. In F. D. Harper, ed., *Alcohol Abuse and Black America*. Alexandria, Va.: Douglass Publishers, Inc.

Lasley-James, R. 1992. Age, social context, and street gang membership: Are "youth" gangs becoming "adult" gangs? *Youth and Society* 23, 4:434–451.

Latimer, D., and J. Goldberg. 1981. *Flowers in the Blood: The Story of Opium*. New York: Franklin Watts.

Leis, Philip E. 1964. Palm oil, illicit gin, and the moral order of the Ijaw. *American Anthropologist* 66:828–837.

Levine, M. 1988. An analysis of mutual assistance. *American Journal of Community Psychology* 16:167–188.

Lewis, L. 1931. *Phantastica: Narcotic and Stimulating Drugs and Their Use and Abuse*. Trans. P. H. Wirth. New York: Dutton.

Lincoln, C. E. 1989. Knowing the Black Church: What it does and why. In Janet Dewart, ed., *The State of Black America*. New York: National Urban League, Inc.

Livingstone, D., and C. Livingstone. 1865. *Narrative of an Expedition to the Zambesi and Its Tributaries*. London: John Murray.

Los Angeles Unified School District. 1989. *GREAT: Gang Resistance Education and Training*. Los Angeles: Office of Instruction.

MacRobert, I. 1988. *The Black Roots and White Racism of Early Pentecostalism in the U.S.A.* New York: St. Martin's Press.

Maddahian, E., M. Newcomb, and P. Bentler. 1986. Adolescents' substance use: Impact of ethnicity, income, and availability. *Advances in Alcohol and Substance Abuse* 5, 3:63–78.

———. 1988. Adolescent drug use and intention to use drugs: Concurrent and longitudinal analyses of four ethnic groups. *Addictive Behaviors* 13:191–195.

Maisto, S., M. Galizio, and G. Conners. 1991. *Drug Use and Misuse*. Holt, Rinehart and Winston.

Mannix, D. 1962. *Black Cargoes: A History of the Atlantic Slave Trade*. New York: Viking.

Martinez, F. B. 1992. The impact of gangs and drugs in the community. In R. C. Cervantes, ed., *Substance Abuse and Gang Violence*. Newbury Park, Calif.: SAGE Publications. Pp. 60–73.

Maton, K., and M. Zimmerman. 1992. Psychosocial predictors of substance use among urban black male adolescents. *Drugs and Society* 6, 1–2:79–113.

Mays, B. E., and J. W. Nicholson. 1969 [1933]. *The Negro's Church*. New York: Russell & Russell.

McCoy, A. W. 1972. *The Politics of Heroin in Southeast Asia*. New York: Harper and Row.

McKay, C. 1968. *Harlem: Negro Metropolis*. New York: Harcourt Brace Jovanovich.

Meir, A. 1964. *Negro Thought in America: 1880–1915*. Ann Arbor: University of Michigan Press.

Milburn, N., and J. Booth. 1992. Illicit drug and alcohol use among homeless black adults in shelters. *Drugs and Society* 6, 1-2:115–155.

Morales, A. 1992. A clinical model for the prevention of gang violence and homicide. In R. C. Cervantes, ed., *Substance Abuse and Gang Violence*. Newbury Park, Calif.: SAGE Publications. Pp. 105–118.

Morgan, H. W. 1974. *Yesterday's Addicts: American Society and Drug Abuse, 1865–1910*. Norman: University of Oklahoma Press.

Mortimer, W. G. 1974. *A History of Coca: The Divine Plant of the Incas*. San Francisco: And/Or Press.

Moynihan, D. P. 1965. *The Negro Family: The Case for National Action*. Washington, D.C.: U.S. GPO.

———. 1967. The Negro family: The case for national action. In L. Rainwater and W. L. Yancy, eds., *The Moynihan Report and the Politics of Controversy*. Cambridge, Mass.: M.I.T. Press.

Mukenge, I. R. 1983. *The Black Church in Urban America*. New York: University Press of America.

Musto, D. F. 1973. *The American Disease: Origins of Narcotic Control*. New Haven: Yale University Press.

National Health Interview Study. 1965–1991. Data compiled by the Office on Smoking and Health, Centers for Disease Control and Prevention, 1993.

National Institute on Alcohol Abuse and Alcoholism (NIAAA). 1980. *National Drug and Alcoholism Treatment Utilization Survey: Comprehensive Report*. Rockville, Md.: National Institute on Alcohol Abuse and Alcoholism.

———. 1983. *National Drug and Alcoholism Treatment Utilization Survey. Comprehensive Report*. Rockville, Md.: National Institute on Alcohol Abuse and Alcoholism.

National Institute on Drug Abuse (NIDA). 1990. *National Household Survey on Drug Abuse: Main Findings*. U.S. Department of Health and Human Services. Public Health Service. Alcohol, Drug Abuse, and Mental Health Administration.

———. 1991. *Annual Emergency Room Data: Data from the Drug Abuse Warning Network*. U.S. Department of Health and Human Services. Public Health Service. Alcohol, Drug Abuse, and Mental Health Administration. Division of Epidemiology and Prevention Research. Rockville, Md.

———. 1991. *Drug Use among Youth: Findings from the 1988 National Household Survey on Drug Abuse*. U.S. Department of Health and Human Services. Publication No. (ADM) 91-1765. Washington, D.C.: U.S. GPO.

National Narcotics Intelligence Consumer Committee. 1993. *The NNICC Report, 1993: The Supply of Illicit Drugs to the United States*.

Netting, R. McC. 1964. Beer as a locus of value among the West African Kofyar. *American Anthropologist* 66:375–384.

Newman, R. G. 1977. *Methadone Treatment in Narcotic Addiction*. New York: Academic Press.

O'Donnell, J. A., H. Voss, R. Clayton, G. Slatin, and R. Room. 1976. *Man and Drugs: A Nationwide Survey*. Research Monograph, Vol. 5. Rockville, Md.: National Institute on Drug Abuse.

Opium Poppy Control Act 1942 (Chapter 720, December 11, 1942). 56 United States Statutes At Large, pp. 1045–1049.

Population of the United States in 1860; Compiled from the Original Returns of the Eighth Census of the United States. Washington, D.C.: U.S. GPO.

Porche-Burke, L., and C. Fulton. 1992. The impact of gang violence: Strategies for prevention and intervention. In R. C. Cervantes, ed., *Substance Abuse and Gang Violence*. Newbury Park, Calif.: SAGE Publications. Pp. 85–104.

Prothrow-Stith, D. 1991. *Deadly Consequences: How Violence Is Destroying Our Teenage Population and a Plan to Begin Solving the Problem*. New York: HarperCollins.

Quarles, B. 1987. *The Negro in the Making of America*. New York: Macmillan.

Ratner, M. *Crack Pipe as Pimp: An Eight-City Ethnographic Study of the Sex-for-crack Phenomenon*. Silver Spring, Md.: Birch and Davis Associates.

Ray, O., and C. Ksir. 1990. *Drugs, Society, and Human Behavior*. Boston: Times Mirror/Mosby College Publishing.

Report of the Secretary's Task Force on Black and Minority Health. 1986. Vol. 7: *Chemical Dependency and Diabetes*. U.S. Office of Minority Health, Department of Health and Human Services. Washington, D.C.: U.S. GPO.

Roberts, H. B. 1987. *The Inner World of the Black Juvenile Delinquent*. Hillsdale, N.J.: Erlbaum.

Robins, L. N., P. A. West, and B. L. Herjanic. 1975. Arrests and delinquency in two generations: A study of Black urban families and their children. *Journal of Child Psychology and Psychiatry* 16:125–140.

Roper, W. L. 1991. Opening keynote address: The prevention of minority youth violence must begin despite risks and imperfect understanding. *Journal of the U.S. Public Health Service* 106:229–231.

Rorabaugh, W. J. 1979. *The Alcoholic Republic*. New York: Oxford University Press.

Royce, J. 1981. *Alcohol Problems and Alcoholism: A Comprehensive Survey*. New York: Free Press.

Santos, R. L. 1991. One approach to oversampling Blacks and Hispanics: The national alcohol survey. In W. B. Clark and M. E. Hilton, eds., *Alcohol in America: Drinking Practices and Problems*. Albany: State University NY Press. Pp. 329–344.

Schaef, A. 1987. *When Society Becomes an Addict*. San Francisco: Harper and Row.

Scott, B. M., R. W. Denniston, and K. M. Magruder. 1992. Alcohol advertising in the African American community. *Journal of Drug Issues* 22, 2:455–469.

Sellers, J. 1943. *The Prohibition Movement in Alabama*. Chapel Hill, N.C.: University of North Carolina Press.

Shakur, S. 1993. *Monster: The Autobiography of an L.A. Gang Member.* New York: Atlantic Monthly Press.

Sinclair, A. 1962. *Era of Excess.* New York: Harper and Row.

Smith, W. B. 1838 (1967). The persimmon tree and the beer dance. In B. Jackson, ed., *The Negro and His Folklore in 19th-Century Periodicals.* Austin: University of Texas Press.

Solomon, D., ed. 1966. *The Marijuana Papers.* New York: Signet Books.

Sorer, H., ed. 1992. *Acute Cocaine Intoxication: Current Methods of Treatment.* NIDA Research Monograph Series No. 123.

Spaights, E., and G. Simpson. 1986. Some unique causes of Black suicide. *Psychology: A Quarterly Journal of Human Behavior* 23, 1:1–5.

Spergel, I. A., R. E. Ross, G. D. Curry, and R. Chance. 1989. *Survey of Youth Gang Problems and Programs in 45 Cities and 6 States.* Washington, D.C.: Office of Juvenile Justice and Delinquency Prevention.

Spiro, M. 1966. Religion: Problems of definition and explanation. In M. Banton, ed., *Anthropological Approaches to the Study of Religion.* London: Tavistock.

Spunt, B. J., P. J. Goldstein, P. A. Belluci, and T. Miller. 1990. *Journal of Psychoactive Drugs* 22:293–303.

Stampp, K. 1961. *The Peculiar Institution: Slavery in the Ante-Bellum South.* New York: Alfred A. Knopf.

Steer, R. A., and B. F. Shaw. (1977). Structure of depression in Black alcoholics. *Psychological Reports* 41, 1235–1241.

Strickland, D., and T. Finn. 1984. Targeting of magazine alcohol beverage advertisements. *Journal of Drug Issues* 14, 3:449–467.

Strickland, D., T. Finn, and M. Lambert. 1982. Content analysis of beverage alcohol advertising, magazine advertising. *Journal of Studies on Alcohol* 43, 7: 655–682.

Taylor, J., and B. Jackson. 1990, December. Factors affecting alcohol consumption in black women. Part 2. *International Journal of the Addictions* 25, 12: 1415–1427.

Terry, C. E., and M. Pellens. 1928. *The Opium Problem.* New York: Bureau of Social Hygiene.

Terry, W. 1984. *Bloods: An Oral History of the Vietnam War by Black Veterans.* New York: Ballantine Books.

Thornberry, T. P., M. D. Krohn, A. J. Lizotte, and D. Chard-Wierschem. 1993. The role of juvenile gangs in facilitating delinquent behavior. *Journal of Research in Crime and Delinquency* 30, 1:55–87.

Thrasher, F. M. 1963. *The Gang.* Chicago: University of Chicago Press. (Originally published in 1927.)

United Nations Department of Social Affairs. 1953. *Bulletin of Narcotics* 5:3–4.

United States Census Office. 1886. *Tenth Census 1880.* Vol. 2. Vital Statistics of the United States. Washington, D.C.: U.S. GPO.

———. 1920. *Fourteenth Census of the United States.* Washington, D.C.: U.S. GPO.

———. 1940. *Sixteenth Census of the United States.* Washington, D.C.: U.S. GPO.

———. 1960. *The Eighteenth Census of Population of the United States.* Washington, D.C.: U.S. GPO.

————. 1990. *The Twenty-first Census of the United States.* Washington, D.C.: U.S. GPO.

United States Department of Education. 1992. *What Works: Schools without Drugs.* National Clearinghouse for Alcohol and Drug Information. Rockville, Md.

United States Department of Justice. 1990. *Drug Use Forecasting: Drugs and Crime.* Office of Justice Programs. National Institute of Justice. Washington, D.C.

————. 1993. *Drug Use Forecasting.* Annual Report. Drugs and Crime in America's Cities. Office of Justice Programs. National Institute of Justice.

————. 1990. *Uniform Crime Reports: 1990.* Washington, D.C.: U.S. GPO.

————. 1991. *Uniform Crime Reports: 1991.* Federal Bureau of Investigation. Release date August 30, 1992. Washington, D.C.: U.S. GPO.

United States Drug Enforcement Administration. 1993a. *Illegal Drug Price/Purity Report. United States. January 1989 through September 1992.*

————. 1993b. *Worldwide Cocaine Situation Report.* 1992. Drug Intelligence Report. Annual.

VanDyke, H. B. 1949. New analgesic drugs. *Bulletin of the New York Academy of Sciences* 25:152–175.

Vogel, V. H., H. Isbell, and K. W. Chapman. 1948. Present status of narcotic addiction. *Journal of the American Medical Association* 138:1019–1026.

Wallace, B. C. 1991. *Crack Cocaine: A Practical Treatment Approach for the Chemically Dependent.* New York: Brunner/Mazel.

————. 1993. Cross cultural counseling with the chemically dependent: Preparing for service delivery within a culture of violence. *Journal of Psychoactive Drugs* 25, 1:9–20.

Washington, G., and W. Beasley. 1988. Black religion and the affirmation of complementary polarity. *Western Journal of Black Studies* 12:142–147.

Watts, W., and L. Wright. 1990. The relationship of alcohol, tobacco, marijuana, and other illegal drug use to delinquency among Mexican-American, black, and white adolescent males. *Adolescence* 25, 97:171–181.

Weir, S. 1985. *Qat in Yemen: Consumption and Social Change.* London: British Museum Publications.

Welte, J., and G. Barnes. 1987. Alcohol use among adolescent minority groups. *Journal of Studies on Alcohol* 48, 4:329–336.

Whitener, D. 1945. *Prohibition in North Carolina, 1715–1945.* Chapel Hill, N.C.: University of North Carolina Press.

William, T. 1989. *The Cocaine Kids.* Reading, Mass.: Addison Wesley Publishing Company.

Williams, C. 1992. *No Hiding Place: Empowerment and Recovery for Our Troubled Communities.* San Francisco: Harper.

Wilmore, G. S. 1972. *Black Religion and Black Radicalism.* Garden City, N.Y.: Doubleday.

Zimmerman, M., and K. Maton. 1992. Lifestyle and substance use among male African American urban adolescents: A cluster analytic approach. *American Journal of Community Psychology* 20, 1:121–138.

INDEX

Cocaine Outreach and Recovery Program (CORP), xiii, 103; approach, x, xi, 110–112; historical background, 140–141
Coca leaves, 90, 91, 92, 94
Codeine, 77
Cognitive-affective impairment, 51
Colleges and universities: church-founded, 136; members who use drugs, 32; 1960's drug use at, 25–26; post–Civil War period, 11
Colombia, 28–29, 94, 95
Color blindness of white therapists, 44
Community leadership, 27. *See also* Churches
Compliance: counterproductive effect of, x–xi, 102, 111; of white therapists, 44
Comprehensive Drug Abuse Prevention and Control Act, 60
Confessions of an English Opium Eater, 77
Coors, 54, 55
Coping. *See* Emotional survival
CORP. *See* Cocaine Outreach and Recovery Program
Counseling: barriers by white therapists, 43–44; outreach, 48, 56
Crack cocaine, 26, 89, 96–117, 125; case studies, 72, 73, 98–99, 115–116; design of the treatment program, 109–115; epidemic, current status, 30–32; epidemic, historical background, ix, 27–29, 30, 117; mass marketing of, 17; origin of, 28; progression of addiction, 28, 96–97, 108–109; psychological aspects, 103–106; purity of, 96; relapse, 106–107; related physical problems, 102–103; treatment, 99–107; use by arrestees, 31
Crime, 27, 123–124; arrest rates, 128–129; guns and gun injuries, 71, 72, 74, 129; risk factors for youth, 127–128; by youth, 128–131. *See also* Drug dealing; Prostitution; Violence

Crips, 122–123, 130
Cultural factors: in chemical dependency, 41–44; of crack cocaine addicts, 110, 112, 113; diversity among African Americans, 33–34; influence of churches, 143–144; marijuana use and, 75

Dangerous Drug Act, 86
DAWN, 64, 97
DEA, 28
Dealers. *See* Drug dealing
Death of a Race conference, 138
Department of Justice, 31
Depression, 42, 51, 67, 68, 104
Depression, The Great, 17–18
De Quincey, Thomas, 77
Dere's No Hidin' Place Down There, 89
Detoxification. *See* Withdrawal
Discrimination, 34, 41, 43, 135
Dole, Vincent P., 83, 84
Domestic violence, 69, 70, 73, 98
Douglass, Frederick, 136
Dreser, Heinrich, 78
Dropouts, 43, 62
Drug Abuse Warning Network (DAWN), 64, 97
Drug addiction: behavior of addicts, 42, 101–103; British system for management of, 86–87; churches and, 134–146; crack cocaine *vs.* heroin and alcohol, 108–109; as a disease, 84, 112, 117; for emotional survival, 10–11, 20, 66, 86; ethnic perception of, ix–x; four associative factors, 88; identifying the addict, 101–103; patterns of, 148; post–Civil War to WWII, 11–18; predisposition to, 66; relapse, 106–107. *See also individual drugs;* Military use of drugs
Drug dealing, 21, 71, 83; crack cocaine, 89, 97, 100–101, 104; distributers, 89; by gangs, 124, 125, 126; as source of drugs, 72; as source of income, 12, 21, 36, 43, 70, 148

Negro Convention Movement, 136
Negro Independence Movement, 137
Newton, John, 134
New York City Ambulatory Detoxifi-
cation Program, 84
New York Urban League, 21
NIAAA, 48
Nicotine. *See* Cigarettes
NIDA, 63, 85
Nightmares, 67
Night sweats, 68
Nyswander, Marie, 83, 84

O'Day, Anita, 93
Office of Economic Opportunity, 20
One Day at a Time program, 100
Operation Golden Flow, 22
Operation PUSH, 58
Opiates, 76–88; geographic origin of
addicts, 1935–1966, 82; use by
arrestees, 32, 63
Opium, 77–78; 1920–1960, 17, 24,
38; anti-drug legislation, 13, 78,
79; post–Civil War period, 12, 13;
trade of, 12, 14, 76, 77, 78, 79
Opium Poppy Control Act of 1942, 78
Opium Wars, 12, 14, 78
Original Gangsters, 123
Outreach counseling, 48, 55–56
Overdose, 86

Paternalism of white therapists, 44
PCP, 25, 73, 74
*Peculiar Institution: Slavery in the Ante-
Bellum South, The*, 10
Pemberton, John Styth, 91
Personality factors, 42
Peru, 28
Pinochet Ugarte, Augusto, 27
Poverty, 39, 41, 42
Prejudice, 34
Prevention: of drug addiction, 41–44,
52; of gang involvement, 131–132
"Prison hospitals" for heroin addic-
tion, 81, 82
Prohibition era, 15–17, 36–37,
82–83

Prostitution, 64, 85, 86; crack co-
caine and, 98, 99, 101, 105
Pryor, Richard, 94
Psychological factors, 42, 103–106,
107, 108, 109–110, 145
Public Health Service, 79, 81
Puerto Ricans, 21, 83, 93, 98
Pulmonary disorders, 102, 108
Pure Food and Drug Act of 1906,
14, 92

Qat, 5
Quarterly Journal of Inebriety, 91

Racism, 27, 34, 137; alcohol abuse
and, 42–44; internalized, 49; in le-
gal system, ix, 13, 38; post-WWII
return to, 18; Prohibition era, 16, 35
Rape, 54, 74, 75, 128–129
Really the Blues, 93
Reconstruction movement, 11
Recovery. *See* Drug treatment pro-
grams; Methadone maintenance
programs; Withdrawal
Relapse, 106–107, 116. *See also*
Money; Sexual behavior
Religions. *See* Churches
Research needs, 147–148
R. J. Reynolds Tobacco Company, 59
Rock houses, 30, 115, 126
Role models, 88, 127
Rucker, Eddie, 37
Rush, Benjamin, 15
Rushing, Jimmy, 35

Segregation, 12, 38, 48, 135; in
the military, 18, 23–24; in the
South, 16
Self-esteem, xi, 42, 51, 61, 106, 108
Serturner, Frederich, 77, 78
Sexual abuse, 113
Sexual behavior: alcohol advertising
promoting, 53–54; effect of crack
cocaine on, 101, 105–106, 107,
113, 114; effect of recovery on, 68
Sexually transmitted diseases, 105.
See also HIV/AIDS

study, 44–47; drug use by arrestees, 31, 32, 63, 97; in gangs, 124; opiate addiction, 13, 82; perceptions concerning during Prohibition, 15, 16; sexual exploitation of, xi, 105, 113

Women and Crack-Cocaine, 93

World War I, 16, 17

World War II, 18, 82

Wright, Alder, 78

Yesterday's Addicts, 92

Young Life Campaign, 21

Youth: advertising of alcohol and, 52–54; alcohol use, 50–52; child abuse/neglect, 98, 105; cigarette use, mean age of initial, 58; cocaine powder use, 1960's, 93; crack cocaine, 98, 99; heroin use, 1950's, 83; leading cause of death, 121; marijuana use, 64–66; percent not gang members, 123; risk factors in drug use, 65; runaways, 74; violence and, 128–131. *See also* Gangs; Prostitution